India

Berlitz Publishing Company, Inc.

Princeton   Mexico City   Dublin   Eschborn   Singapore

Original Text: Jack Altman
Editor: Media Content Marketing, Inc.
Photography: © Nick Sumner 1998 (pages 3, 5, 6, 10–11, 13,
                    14, 16, 18, 23, 43, 76–77, 93, 102–103, 110,
                    124, 134–135, 136, 148–149, 152, 156,
                    172–173, 204, 205, 206); Walter Imber (pages 4,
                    8, 9, 19, 21, 22, 29, 30, 32, 35, 36, 39, 46, 49,
                    52, 54–55, 59, 60, 62, 65, 66–67, 68, 70, 80, 86,
                    89, 91, 92, 94, 97, 99, 100, 101,105, 107, 108,
                    111, 112–113, 116, 118–119, 122, 127, 129,
                    132, 141, 143, 144, 146, 151, 154–155,
                    158–159, 161, 163, 165, 167, 170, 174,
                    176–177, 179, 180, 182–183, 184–185, 186,
                    189, 190, 195, 196, 198–199, 201, 202–203,
                    211, 212, 214–215, 216, 217, 219, 221, 222);
                    and © India Tourist Board (pages 40, 72, 83)
Photo Editor: Naomi Zinn
Layout: Media Content Marketing, Inc.
Cartography: Ortelius Design

*Although the publisher tries to insure the accuracy of all the infor-
mation in this book, changes are inevitable and errors may result.
The publisher cannot be responsible for any resulting loss, incon-
venience, or injury. If you find an error in this guide, please let the
editors know by writing to Berlitz Publishing Company, 400
Alexander Park, Princeton, NJ 08540-6306.*

ISBN 2-8315-7050-6
Revised 1999 – First Printing March 1999

Printed in Italy
019/903 REV

CONTENTS

● A (☛ in the text denotes a highly recommended sight

India

INDIA AND ITS PEOPLE

This land is a constant challenge to mind and body, a glorious shock to the system. It is no place for the faint-hearted. India is exhilarating, exhausting, and infuriating—a land where, you'll find, the practicalities of daily life overlay the mysteries that popular myth attaches to India. In place of the much-publicized, and much-misunderstood, mysticism of its ancient religions, India in reality has quite another miracle to offer in the sheer profusion of its peoples and landscapes.

India comprises a diamond-shaped subcontinent that stretches over 3,000 km (1,800 miles) from the Kashmir mountains in the north right down to Kanyakumari, or Cape Comorin, on the Indian Ocean. From east to west India also covers about 3,000 km, from Arunachal Pradesh and Assam on the border with its neighbors China and Burma to the Gujarat coast on the Arabian Sea. Only in more recent post-colonial times did its natural geography exclude the countries of Pakistan and Bangladesh. Even there, for all the hostilities, there's an undeniable cultural affinity with India—feuding brothers rather than unrelated strangers. In fact, when you look at its 4,000 years of history—or any of today's newspapers, for that matter—its countless feuds seem to be a perpetual but necessary dynamic of Indian civilization.

India is a massive family, with a lot of different and inevitably conflicting regional and sectarian interests. Rupee banknotes are printed in India's 15 official languages: Hindi, Urdu, Sanskrit, Sindhi, Bengali, Marathi, Gujurati, Oriya, Punjabi, Assamese, Kashmiri, and Malayalam, as well as Kannada, Tamil, and Telugu. A count of the languages spoken all over India, leaving out the dialects, comes to 1,652, written in 13 different alphabets.

The national language of Hindi is spoken by less than the majority, and English, for which the government has a permanent program of modernization, is spoken by just 3 percent of the people, mostly in the largest cities. Everybody "speaks" cricket, though, with its *innings*, *wickets*, and *boundaries* present in every dialect.

One of the first impressions you'll get at the airport in Delhi or Mumbai (Bombay) is the diversity of ethnic types. From blue-eyed and sometimes red-haired Kashmiris and the Chinese-Tibetans from Sikkim or Darjeeling, through all the shades of coffee of the heartland, right down to dark-skinned, often curly-haired, Dravidians from southern India, you soon realize there's no such thing as a "typical" Indian.

India's prehistoric settlers were probably what anthropologists call Proto-Australoids. They've since been joined by Mongols, Aryans, Greeks, Arabs, Turks, Persians, and Afghans, while Dutch, British, Portuguese, and French have also left their traces.

The landscape is alternately rich and arid, lush and desolate. The majestic Himalayas in the north make an appropriate home for Shiva, one of the most-revered Hindu gods. Kashmir is a serenely beautiful and coveted land of green forest, alpine meadows, and lakes, while the Punjab in the northwest is the fertile center of the country's Green Revolution, supporting the nation's self-sufficiency in wheat, barley, and millet. On the doorstep of this wealth, the Thar Desert of noble Rajasthan heralds the vast Deccan plateau of parched, ruddy granite that dominates the peninsula of southern India.

Delhi stands at the western end of the Ganga (Ganges) river basin in which India grows

South Indian carving inspired artists throughout all of Southeast Asia.

Bihari rice workers tend to the far-stretching fields which provide India with a good deal of its sustenance.

much of its rice. Flanked with patches of forest leading up into the foothills of the Himalayas, the flat plain stretches right across to the Bay of Bengal 1,600 km (1,000 miles) away, but some areas are kept as nature reserves for the country's wildlife, notably its tigers, leopards, and elephants. Bengal's greenery is the threshold to the tea plantations of Darjeeling and Assam.

The rugged southern peninsula is hemmed in by low-lying mountains—the Vindhya and Satpura to the north and the Western and Eastern Ghats running parallel to the coasts. The forested Malabar coast in the west is sown with crops of coconut, betel-nut, pepper, rubber, and cashew nut, which today still tempt ships across the Arabian Sea. Some of the palm trees in the area provide shade for beach resorts in Goa and Kerala.

India's landscape also features man-made architectural treasures, bearing witness to the many great religions and civilizations which have enriched the country—monuments now, after centuries of neglect, preserved by the restoration program started by the Archaeological Survey of India. The sights are endless: the Hindu *gopuram* tower-gates of the south, the temples of Varanasi (Benares), the cave monasteries of Ajanta and Ellora, the beautiful and erotic sculptures of Khajuraho, the splendid marble palaces, fortresses, and mausoleums of the emperors and maharajas in Delhi, Agra, and Rajasthan, the colonial government buildings in New Delhi, or the unusual style of the Gothic-Oriental railway station in Mumbai (known until 1995 as Bombay).

The cities' shanty-town districts are often directly in the shadow of the shining skyscrapers, built by the shanty-town residents themselves. Here women carry bricks on their heads as gracefully as a pitcher of water. The women are also responsible for one other characteristic of Indian "architecture"—cow-dung patties which are preserved and kept for fuel and artfully shaped into mounds with shapes that differ from region to region, some of them resembling a Buddhist *stupa*, a Hindu *gopuram,* or even a Moslem minaret.

The ancient city of Varanasi exemplifies the striking beauty and mystery of India as a whole.

The only constant in this huge landscape is the people them-selves. Even in the vast open spaces of the Rajasthan desert or the Deccan plateau of central India, people appear everywhere, a tribesman on camel-back or lone woman holding her headdress in her teeth to keep out the dust as she carries a huge pitcher of water or a bundle of firewood on her head. If, as the road stretches before you empty and clear right up to the horizon, and you can see only one tree, it's a pretty safe bet you'll find at least one *sadhu* (holy man) resting in its shade.

The teeming millions living in Calcutta and Mumbai have become legendary. They crowd each other into the roadway, bulge out of tiny auto-rickshaws, and perch on top of buses and trains; a family of four or five clings onto a motor-scooter, and a whole school class on one bullock-cart. It's hazardous; buses do topple over, rooftop passengers on trains do occasionally get swept off the top by an overhanging steel rod, but they accept the risk for the free ride—rooftoppers aren't in the habit of buying tickets.

It's important to remember not to apply Western values to everything you see here. The poverty, for instance, does not create the sense of shame as it does for people who live in Western countries. In India poverty is borne with considerable dignity and even with a cheerfulness that some may find difficult to understand. The same form applies to jostling, which is a whole way of life in this country.

Everyone makes way for the cow, sacred to the Hindus. The cow has right of way everywhere, whether walking nonchalantly through the center of a city, or reclining across a new expressway. After a while you may begin to detect something a bit uncanny in the way a cow seems to look around and beyond her immediate surroundings — it's as if she *knows* that she's sacred.

You can't get around it: India is a country where religion is ever-present. Although the constitution of today describes India as a secular State, religion still plays a vital part in everyday life—in its streets as well as in the architecture, sculpture, and painting of its great monuments. A little background information on the major forms of faith may help.

Religions of India

Hinduism

If **Hinduism** is more or less India's national belief system, this may be because it offers something for everyone: mysticism and metaphysics for scholars, ceremony for ordinary people, austerity, sensuality, tranquillity, and frenzy.

Building on the ancient cults and Vedic teachings of the Indo-Aryans dating from 1300 B.C., Hinduism began to take its present form in the fourth century A.D., under considerable pressure for a more "accessible" religion. Popular devotional worship, with its appeal to the common people, replaced the sacrifices practiced exclusively by the Brahmins.

It is said there are 330 million gods in the Hindu pantheon, but they might be seen as 330 million facets of a single divinity. The three most important manifestations of the Brahman, or godhead, are Vishnu, Brahma, and Shiva, which are often presented to Westerners as a trinity, though this is not really comparable to the Christian concept.

The "big three" are by no means accorded equal status. Vishnu, the preserver, is regarded by his worshippers as a god from whose navel a lotus grew bearing Brahma whose task it was to create the

These Rajasthani women from western India are proud descendants of rulers and warriors.

A proud owner at the Pushkar Fair, where camels, horses, and bullocks are brought from everywhere to be sold at market.

world. Vishnu, a four-armed god with mace, conch, discus, and lotus, has many incarnations, of which the most famous is Krishna, who appears as conquering hero, flute-playing lover, or mischievous baby. Vishnu's wife Lakshmi is goddess of good fortune.

Shiva is the dancing destroyer-god, wearing a garland of skulls and snakes around both neck and arms. As the god of time and ascetics, he decides the fate of the world. As Lord of beasts and king of dance, Shiva is as passionate as Vishnu is serene. Just in case you think you have got it all clear in your mind, remember that Vishnu destroys by not preserving and Shiva preserves through the renewal arising from destruction.

Hindu ethics say that the path to salvation has three principles: righteousness, prosperity honestly achieved, and, not least, pleasure. At the center of the confrontation with the harsh reality of daily life is the concept of *karma*; that is "work" or "deed," and the implication that the sum total of one's acts in a previous life will determine one's present station in life. A better reincarnation is promised those whose deeds and actions are good in this station. The ultimate goal is spiritual salvation, or *moksha*, a freeing from the cycle of rebirth.

While this teaching has served to sustain the rigid hierarchy of the caste system, it is not so "fatalistic" as some would have it. The Hindus say we cannot escape our karma, but that with good judgment and foresight we can use it to our advantage.

By the 19th century, reformers such as the Bengali Brahman Ram Mohan Roy tried to rid Hinduism of primitive idolatry. The self-immolation of widows, known as *sati*—a widow becomes sati, a "virtuous woman," by climbing onto her husband's funeral pyre—has disappeared, but the monkey-god Hanuman and elephant-headed Ganesh are still idolized, and nobody will dare to deny the sanctity of the cow and all her products: milk, curd, butter, and dung, the last of which is used for fuel.

More than 83 percent of the population embraces Hinduism, which is more a way of life than a religion; its sacred rituals and observances are only a small part of what good Hindus believe makes them good Hindus. Much more than the mystical elements which fascinate and draw so many Westerners here, Hinduism is concerned with the basics of everyday life: birth, work, health, relationships, and death, all of this helped along by regular consultations with a local astrologer.

Amritsar's Golden Temple plays the role of both shrine and fortress for beleaguered Sikhs.

Even today, the intricate Hindu caste system can play a role in the Indians' choice of job, spouse, and political party, despite the numerous anti-discrimination statutes passed since Independence. *Brahmins*, the priestly caste, fill many of the top posts in the universities and administration; many Indian Army officers can trace their ancestry to the proud *Kshatriya* warrior caste; business is dominated by the merchant or *Vaishya* caste; and *Shudras* till the land. The so-called Untouchables have greater opportunities now to rise on the social scale, a few of them becoming captains of industry or cabinet ministers, but it's still their brethren who sweep the streets.

Most marriages in India are still arranged traditionally with carefully negotiated dowries. While ever more matrimonial advertise-

ments in the weekend editions of *The Times of India* and other newspapers mention "caste no bar," just as many specify the required
caste or insist on a "fair-complexioned" bride while touting a university diploma or an American work permit.

Islam

Following a conflict in India almost as old as **Islam** itself, a peaceful coexistence between Hinduism and Islam seems hard to
achieve. It's hard to imagine a faith more hostile to all idolatry,
fierce in its uncompromising monotheism, and opposed to the caste
system as Islam When *sufi* mystics or the emperor Akbar tried to
create a synthesis between the two faiths, the orthodox on both
sides resisted.

Hindu conversions to Islamic faith were more often performed
out of hope of social advancement under a Muslim government than
out of conviction. Muslims in India today, as fervent as their
brethren in Pakistan or the Middle East, are mostly descendants of
those converts.

Over 80 million Muslims form the second-largest religious
group in India—almost as many as the population of Pakistan—
most of them descendants from Hindu converts of the Mughals'
empire, who bore the brunt of Hindu retaliation for long years full
of subjection and an often unfair identification with British rule.
Left behind by the exodus to Pakistan at the 1947 partition, they
make up the peasantry in the north. While they mostly keep a low
profile, you may hear of "communal incidents" in the cities between the Hindus and Muslims.

Followers of Islam in India are divided into two primary groups:
Sunnis (adherents of the Sunna law expounded by Mohammed's
own words and deeds) and Shiites (followers of those interpretations
proposed by Mohammed's cousin Ali). Every day, the devout face
Mecca, bow their foreheads to the ground, and proclaim: "There is
no god but Allah; and Mohammed is His Prophet."

Hemis Gompa, a celebration that in its trappings clearly illustrates the Tibetan influence in India.

Sikhs

The one attempt to merge the principles of Hinduism and Islam is that of the **Sikhs** ("disciples"). Nanak, their *guru* (teacher), was born a Hindu in 1469 and reared on the egalitarian principles of Islam. He opposed idolatry and the caste system (which was subsequently too strong to resist). From Islam he took the idea of one God, but refused any such specific conception as Allah. He saw God's manifestation, like Hinduism, as being everywhere in the world He created. Nanak's teachings were written in the *Adi Granth*, which acquired for Sikhs the sanctity of the Koran. According to this faith, alcohol and tobacco are forbidden.

The militancy of the Sikhs came about only as Nanak's successors got embroiled in politics—with dire results for the Sikhs—when their leaders challenged the Mughals. After the execution of Guru Tegh Bahadur, his son, Guru Gobind Singh, exalted the faithful to be ever ready for armed defense. They all took the surname Singh, meaning "Lion" (all Sikhs are named Singh, but not all Singhs are Sikhs), and wore a turban and kept the five K's: *kesha* (uncut hair and beard), *kanga* (comb for their hair), *kara* (steel bracelet), *kachha* (soldier's shorts), and *kirpan* (dagger). Their distinctive appearance made them highly visible and so inspired an unflinching courage.

Sikhs make up just 2 percent of the population. With the consistent militant need to defend their faith, they make up a fiercely competent élite in the Indian Army, but they are also skilled farmers at the spearhead of the Green Revolution in the Punjab, where most of them live. Their rights have been the source of conflicts in the central government.

Buddhism

Buddhism was founded over 2,500 years ago in reaction to Brahmanic orthodoxy, but it practically vanished as an organized religion

The Karmapa sect of Tibetan monks live in exile in the Sikkim region of India.

from the Indian scene by persecution and absorption into the Hindu mainstream. It continues, however, to exert influence on India's spiritual and artistic life to the present day.

Buddha's own life explains his teachings, but the truth is buried in both legend and historical fact. He was born Siddhartha Gautama in a grove of sal trees at Lumbini (just across the Nepalese border) around the year 566 B.C. His mother, who was queen of the Sakyas, is said to have conceived him after dreaming that a magnificent white elephant holding a lotus flower in his trunk had entered her side.

Siddhartha grew up in princely luxury, but when he was taken out one day to the edge of the royal parks, he saw the poor, the sick, and the aged. Then he saw a religious beggar who seemed serene, and he realized the path his life must take.

Abandoning his riches, Siddhartha went off into the kingdoms of the Ganga valley. For six years he begged for his food, learned to meditate, and practiced severe self-mortification, but still felt no nearer to understanding life's suffering. Then, aged 35, sitting under a tree at the place now known as Bodh Gaya (south of Patna), he vowed to stay there until his goal was achieved.

For 49 days he resisted demons and temptresses, and became truly Enlightened—Buddha as he is called today. He preached his new wisdom at Sarnath (near Varanasi) and with ever more disciples went out to spread his word. Buddha himself converted ruthless bandits and whole armies from the path of violence. In Kushinagar, between Bodh Gaya and his birthplace, he died at age 80 of dysentery, it is said, from eating pork.

Preaching that suffering came from the pursuit of personal desire, Buddha had advocated the Middle Way of the Eightfold Path: right views, right resolve, right speech, right conduct, right livelihood, right effort, right recollection, and right meditation. Only thus could the enlightenment of Nirvana be achieved.

This original doctrine, without any sense of Buddha's divinity, was embraced by the Hinayana (Lesser Vehicle) school which spread to Sri Lanka, Burma, and Thailand, as well as Cambodia and Laos. The Mahayana (Great Vehicle) school added the concept of Bodhisattva as divine savior, and was then the most dominant form of Buddhism, spreading to China and Japan.

After centuries of almost total eclipse, Buddhism today has been able to achieve a revival in India, in part by offering its egalitarian philosophy to Hindu Untouchables as an escape from discrimination. There are now more than 5 million Buddhists in India, many of them in Maharashtra.

Jainism

As old as Buddhism, **Jainism** has made its mark with its concept of *ahimsa* (non-violence) and is much more pacifist than its name, which means religion of the conquerors.

Over two million Indians practice Jainism: their belief in non-violence protects the life of even the humblest fly.

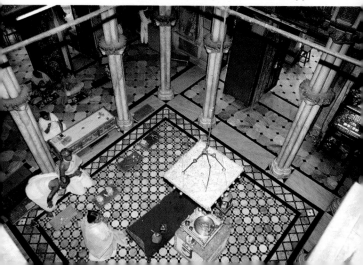

Vardhamana Mahavira was its founder. He was born in 540 B.C. in Bihar and, like Buddha, was the son of a chief. He, too, abandoned riches to become an ascetic. But Mahavira (the Great Hero) pursued self-mortification to the end of his life, stripping off his clothes to take his word from kingdom to kingdom. He died of self-inflicted starvation at the age of 72 in Para, near Rajgir. His followers were later to divide into the *Digambaras* ("space-clad," i.e., naked) and the *Svetambaras* ("white-clad") you see today.

The religion, in which Mahavira is seen as the manifestation of 24 *Tirthankaras* (teachers), attributes souls to all living creatures, as well as other natural objects. Agriculture was therefore abandoned for its destruction of plant and animal life. The doctrines survive in vegetarianism, with Jain monks carrying dusters to sweep insects away from where they tread and wearing a gauze veil over their mouth to avoid breathing in flies.

Jainism, which never spread beyond India, claims 2 million followers, including many businessmen in Gujarat and the Deccan, with a few in Bengal. It had considerable influence on Mahatma Gandhi's non-violence movement; he used its fasting-unto-death as a potent moral and political weapon. The Jains' non-violent religion excludes them from agriculture as a profession, but they dominate the electronics industry in Bangalore.

Parsis, Jews, and Christians

The tiny but powerful community of **Parsis** brought Zoroastrianism from Iran, and its people shine in business today. The Parsis, as their name suggests, originate from ancient Persia and today form only a minute community in the world of religions, with barely 100,000 living in India, mostly in and around the city of Mumbai. They have been and are still enormously influential in this country's

The Jain faith is as intricate as the maze of pillars in this exquisite temple on Mount Abu.

economic life, often serving as all-important go-betweens in the sometimes immensely difficult relations between Hindus and Muslims, and between India and Pakistan.

Their religion dates as far back as the seventh century B.C., when their prophet Zoroaster contrasted his peaceful and sedentary People of Righteousness with the polytheistic nomadic People of Evil. His was an attitude that probably determined not only their general ethics, but also their occupational destiny as highly sophisticated businessmen.

The Parsis base their elaborate code of ethics on the concept of a constant struggle existing between the forces of creation—that is, light and good—and those of darkness and evil. Its teachings puts great emphasis on the very purity of the world's natural elements, fire, earth, and water. For instance, to avoid polluting the elements, Parsis do not bury or cremate their dead, but lay them exposed and naked on their famous Towers of Silence for the vultures to devour.

India's **Jewish** community is ancient indeed. Some texts claim that the first Jews arrived in India at the time of the Babylonian exile, in 587 B.C.; others bring them to Cranganur, on the Malabar coast, in A.D. 72, about the time that the disciple Thomas is thought to have brought his Christian mission to India. The oldest Jewish community still in existence is situated down the coast at Cochin (see page 182), dating back at least to the fourth century A.D. Some others, less orthodox, can be found in Mumbai, but most emigrated to Israel when it was founded in the year 1948.

The earliest **Christians** other than St. Thomas (see page 197), were the so-called Nestorian "heretics" of the Syrian Orthodox Church, also living on the Malabar coast since the first centuries of the Christian era. Modern Indian Christians, some descended from the Syrians, others from those converted by British and Portuguese missionaries, number about 19 million. They are mainly Catholics, living in Goa, and elsewhere you will find all the British variations on Protestantism, all with a certain Hindu tinge to them.

The Zanskari people of northern India celebrate in traditional costume.

The new religion of India is of course modernization, and young, upwardly mobile professionals are everywhere. Growing involvement in electronics, telecommunications, nuclear power, and space satellites is intended to take the country, as one official said, "directly from the 19th into the 21st century." To achieve this transition, the government is cutting through bureaucracy to break with political corruption and find some kind of peaceful *modus vivendi* for communal and regional interests. Former US ambassador John Kenneth Galbraith called it a "functioning anarchy." The miracle of how it functions is well worth observing.

FACTS AND FIGURES

Geography: India's area of 3,287,263 sq km (1,269,212 sq miles) makes it the seventh largest country in the world. It stretches 3,214 km (1,997 miles) from Kashmir south to Cape Comorin on the Indian Ocean, and 2,933 km (1,823 miles) from the eastern frontier with China and Burma to the Gujarat coast on the Arabian Sea. The Himalayas mark the northern frontier, leading down to the plain of the Ganga river stretching east to the Bay of Bengal. In the northeast, Cherrapunji holds the record for the world's heaviest rainfall in a single year, 22,990 mm (905 inches) in 1861. The triangular Deccan plateau of the southern peninsula is flanked by the Vindhya and Satpura mountains to the north and the Eastern and Western Ghats which run parallel to the Coromandel and Malabar coasts. Highest mountain: Kanchenjunga (Sikkim) 8,586 m (28,168 ft).

Population: 935.7 million, of whom 72% are Indo-Aryan, mostly in north, 25% Dravidian in south, 3% others. Density is 273 people per square kilometer (685 per square mile).

Capital: Delhi, pop. 11,300,000

Major cities: Mumbai (once Bombay), pop. 15,000,000; Calcutta, pop. 12,000,000; Hyderabad, pop. 4,900,000; Bangalore, pop. 5,200,000; Chennai (once Madras), pop. 5,900,000; Ahmedabad, pop. 3,600,000; Pune, pop. 2,800,000; and Kanpur, pop. 2,470,000.

Government: India is a republic of 25 states, with seven union territories governed from Delhi. A member of the British Commonwealth, it has parliamentary government established by the 1950 constitution. The President has limited responsibility, real power being vested in a Prime Minister and Council of Ministers responsible to the 544 members of the Lok Sabha (House of the People). State government is in the hands of Chief Ministers and State legislatures, which is represented centrally by a 244-member Rajya Sabha (the Council of States).

Religion: 82.6% Hindu, 11.4% Muslim, 2.4% Christian, 2% Sikh, 1.6% Buddhist, Jain, and others.

A BRIEF HISTORY

India has always been a melange of peoples. Apart from some pre-Ice Age hominids, the first settlers to arrive in India were Negritos and Proto-Australoids. Migrants of Mediterranean stock from the Middle East and Asia seem to have made up the Dravidians, now principally in the southern peninsula.

In 4000 B.C. agriculturalists made their first appearance up in the hills of Baluchistan in the northwest. In the Indus river valley, improved techniques permitted the storage of wheat and barley beyond daily needs, and so the cities of Harappa and Mohenjodaro emerged in the year 2300 B.C., creating a civilization even more advanced than that of the Aryans who came later.

The sewage system and houses outside the citadel were better constructed than their modern equivalents, and among their animals was a major Indian contribution to the world's cuisine—the chicken.

Modern archaeology suggests that this Indus Valley civilization was destroyed not by Aryan conquerors, but by floods, when the Indus river changed course, perhaps due to earthquakes, in about 1700 B.C.

The Hindus' Ancestors

The Aryans arrived on the scene some 200 years later. Originally from Russia or Asia, they migrated to Mesopotamia first and then on to Iran before entering India. These fair-skinned cattle-breeders, who saw the cow as an especially sacred animal, cultivated agriculture in the Punjab after waging war against the Dasas, who then became their slaves.

Early events surrounding the Indo-Aryans can be deduced from the later writings of the *Rig-Veda* (priestly hymns), *Puranas* (ancient tales of kings and gods), and the epic poems of the *Mahabharata* and *Ramayana*. These provided the basis for Hinduism; also, the epics' heroic battles suggest there was a prolonged struggle for land rights over the fertile plains north and east of modern Delhi, followed by invasions and wars.

If ancient writings give only a romanticized view, they do offer a more precise picture of Indo-Aryan society. Their long wars against the indigenous people established their leaders as kings with a hereditary divinity, which the Brahmins (the priests) exchanged for a privileged position of their own. The caste system was already taking shape. Before the conquests, the Aryans were organized in three classes: warriors, priests, and commoners. Then they established four distinct categories known as *varna* (literally, "color").

As possessors of magical power associated with ritual sacrifice and sacred utterance, Brahmins were the sole interpreters of the Vedic scriptures. They laid down a social pecking order with themselves in first place, followed by Kshatriyas (the warriors), Vaishyas (cultivators or traders), and Shudras (serfs and those of mixed blood). This organization became more elaborate as the division of labor became more complicated, so the growing number of occupational groups were subsequently defined as *jati* (subcastes), often living in separate villages. Each caste would preserve its "purity" by avoiding intermarriage and not sharing food with other castes. Outside these were the Untouchables, those of aboriginal descent.

By 600 B.C., the Indo-Aryans had formed monarchies in the Ganga plain, surrounded by smaller tribes resisting the Brahmanic orthodoxy and its authoritarianism. Within the monarchies, thinkers took to the asceticism which has characterized spiritual life in India. The Brahmins cannily countered this threat by absorbing the new ideas into their teachings. But the tribes were less amenable and so became the breeding ground for two new religions espousing non-violence, Jainism and Buddhism.

While rulers fought for control of the Ganga valley, new invaders appeared at India's frontiers; Cyrus, Emperor of Persia, crossed the Hindu Kush mountains into the Indus valley in 530 B.C. While Brahman and Persian scholars exchanged ideas, the Indians copied the Persian coin system. Rock inscriptions left by Emperor Darius probably inspired the pillar-edicts of Indian Emperor Ashoka in the third century B.C.

The spectacular invasion by Alexander the Great of Macedonia in 326 B.C. ended Persian presence, but apart from opening up trade with Asia Minor and the eastern Mediterranean, the Greeks left no lasting impact on India during the two-year campaign.

Alexander's dreams of a huge empire extending eastwards across the Ganga plain were blocked by mutinous troops fed up with upset stomachs, the harsh terrain, and the tough Indian military opposition. He returned to Babylon, leaving a few governors on the frontier.

Ashoka's Empire

Meanwhile, in the Ganga valley power struggle, Magadha (modern Bihar) emerged as the dominant kingdom. Its ruler, Chandragupta

Ajanta's cave-temples provided refuge from flood and plague for the Buddhist and Jain monks.

The story of India's history has been recorded through the ages on the walls of its holy relics.

Maurya (321–297 B.C.), was also to become the founder of India's first imperial dynasty with Pataliputra (modern Patna), the world's largest city at the time, as its capital.

Chandragupta extended his rule to the northwest with a rigorous campaign against the Greek forces of Seleucus Nikator. It ended in a profitable marriage alliance with the Greeks, but later Chandragupta turned to more sober thoughts: he converted to Jainism, and finally starved to death at the temple of Sravanabelagola.

His son Bindusara combined his father's ambition with a taste for the good life and philosophy. He expanded the empire as far down as

Mysore and stunned the western world by asking King Antiochus for Greek wine, figs, and a sophist. The king was happy to send the wine and figs, but would not, however, consent to Bindusara's last request.

To control land and sea routes to the south, the Mauryas still needed to conquer the eastern kingdom of Kalinga (modern Orissa). The task was left to Bindusara's heir Ashoka (269–232 B.C.), admired by Indians as their greatest ruler, perhaps for his special combination of tough authoritarianism and a high sense of moral righteousness. Ashoka began by killing all his rivals before conquering Kalinga in 260 B.C. This left 100,000 dead, with even more dying from famine and disease, while 150,000 were taken captive.

Famous inscriptions on rocks and pillars everywhere bore testimony to Ashoka's reign. The inscriptions state how "he of gentle visage and beloved of the gods," as he described himself, was filled with remorse and converted to the non-violent teachings of Buddha. But metaphysical implications seem to have interested him less than enforcing a moral example to unite his far-flung subjects in peace and fellowship, under him. To oversee this mass conversion, Ashoka turned the Brahmanic concept of *dharma* (righteousness) into an instrument of public policy, enforced by the Officers of Righteousness he had appointed for this purpose. The imperial administration for this undertaking demanded a huge bureaucracy, with superintendents, accountants, and clerks overseeing commerce, forestry, armory, weights and measures, goldsmiths, prostitutes, ships, cows and horses, elephants, chariots, and infantry. Southern India remained independent, but Ashoka had his hands full with a large empire that now extended as far north as Kashmir and east to Bengal.

In the 50 years that followed Ashoka's death, Mauryan power went into decline. Agriculture was not productive enough to finance the empire's expansion. Also, the unwieldy bureaucracy couldn't keep its loyalties straight, with the too-rapid turnover in rulers vying for Ashoka's throne.

Invaders Galore

After the break-up of the Mauryan empire, new invaders appeared on the northwest frontier. The first to arrive were Bactrian Greeks left in the Afghan hills by Alexander's successors. They were welcomed for their erudite ideas on medicine, astronomy, and astrology.

Joined by Iranian kings known as Pahlavas, the Greeks were overrun in the first century B.C. by bands of Scythian nomads known as the Shakas. They moved on into the Ganga valley when other nomads, the Yueh-chi from Central Asia, swept across the frontier.

Emerging victorious from the struggles between the Yueh-chi and the Shakas, King Kanishka of the Kushan established an empire from the northern half of India and into Central Asia.

Buddhism, founded over 2,500 years ago, has achieved a revival in recent years.

His reign was one of prosperity, making India a trade center between east and west.

Kanishka was a champion of the Mahayana (Great Vehicle) school, which attributed for the first time a quasi-divinity to Buddha; his active patronage of the arts led to the creation of the first bronze and stone sculptures of Buddha.

Buddhist and Jain merchants prospered with the new east–west trade and so were able to finance the magnificently sculpted cave-temples in the Deccan, including those at Ajanta and Ellora. The arts also flourished in India during these early times. Madurai was the lively cultural center for Dravidian artists: poets, actors, singers, musicians, and also dancers who were the precursors of the Hindu *devadasi* temple prostitutes.

Gupta Glory

The Gupta dynasty, founded by the obscure Bihari landowner Chandra Gupta I, rose to power during the fourth century A.D. Marriage-alliance and conquest allowed the Guptas to create an empire from Bengal to the Punjab and from Kashmir to the Deccan.

Samudra Gupta, the warrior of the clan, launched lightning raids through the jungles to snatch the gold of the south. The Guptas also captured the western sea ports and their trade with the Arabs. They turned their noses up at trade with the Romans, but China offered many bounties, such as silk, musk, and amber, in exchange for India's spices, jewels, and perfumes—as well as parakeets for the ladies' boudoirs and monkeys for their cooking pots.

The Gupta empire began to crumble in the fifth century, with the onslaught of the so-called White Huns. They were not clearly linked to Attila's Huns, but their harsh agenda of exterminating Buddhists does suggest an affinity. The White Huns seized the Punjab, Kashmir, and a large portion of the western Ganga plain before being chased out again.

In the seventh century, one strong king, Harshavardhana, reigned for 40 years over northern India, and encouraged Buddhist monks and Brahman priests to participate in philosophical discussions. Sages developed the strict disciplines of yoga and profound metaphysical speculations of Vedanta.

In southern India, power was shared by the Pallavas in Kanchipuram and the Pandyas and Cholas vying for control of Thanjavur (Tanjore). The *bhakti* movement of the Tamils brought a new warmth to the hitherto rigid Brahmanic ritual of Hinduism. The temples of Mahabalipuram were a high point in southern architecture, and it was the

Pallavan artists who influenced—and may have helped to build—the temples at Angkor Wat in Cambodia and Borobudur in Java.

Islam Comes to India

Arab trade with India had long since whetted the appetites of the Muslims; when Indian pirates plundered their ships off the coast of Sind in 711, it provoked the Governor of Chaldea (now Iraq) to send troops with 6,000 horses and 6,000 camels to conquer the Sind rajas and offer the alternative of converting to Islam or death. When it was revealed to the Governor of Chaldea that Hinduism was in fact a serious religion with too many faithful to treat in this way, another solution had to be found: Hindus, along with Parsis who had fled an earlier Muslim persecution in Persia, were given the privileged status of *dhimmi*, dues-paying non-believers.

For nearly 300 years, Islamic conquest in India was confined to this trading community in Sind, but in the tenth century, tribesmen from Turkistan, driven west by Chinese expansion, set up a state at Ghazni and began raids across the border to plunder Hindu temples.

Sweeping through the Punjab and Gujarat across to the western end of the Ganga valley, Mahmud of Ghazni (997–1030) used these raids more to finance his empire in Persia and Turkistan than to set up a permanent foothold in India. Mahmud smashed the infidels' idols and destroyed their temples as he went, but was nonetheless cultured enough to use the booty to build a library, a museum, and a splendid mosque when he got back to Ghazni. If Muslims saw him as a righteous militant and Hindus as a brutal monster, neither denied him his title of "Sword of Islam." In order to understand his ambiguous image, compare him with Europe's heroic crusaders who went on the rampage at about the same time.

There was no concerted Indian response to the invasions because the various kingdoms were busy with wars of their own. The Rajput warrior clans fought each other for control in what is now Rajasthan, the Kathiawar peninsula, and as far east as Khajuraho. The Turco-

This temple in Khajuraho, filled with erotic sculpture, was built by the Rajput Chandellas, a clan that brought vigor to love and war.

Afghan invaders were regarded as a transient phenomenon that would either soon disappear or, just like others before them, be swallowed up by the great subcontinent.

A Sultan for Delhi

At the end of the 12th century, the Turks arrived: Sultan Mohammed of Ghur and his Mameluke (slave) General Qutb-ud-din Aybak seized Ghazni in 1173 and invaded India. The Rajputs made a belated alliance and fought valiantly from one desert fortress to another, but their elephants could not match their opponents' fast horses and Afghan cavalry firing superior crossbows at the gallop. By 1193, the Turks were masters in Peshawar, Lahore, and Delhi. The sultan returned to Ghazni and, leaving Qutb-ud-din in charge,

Qutb-ud-din celebrated his Delhi conquest by building a tower from which he could survey the entire city.

moved east to Bengal, destroying centers of Buddhism such as the University of Nalanda.

After his master's assassination in 1206, Qutb-ud-din proclaimed himself sultan of Delhi, head of India's first Islamic dynasty. The sultanate lasted 320 years, but the new sultan ruled only four years: he died in a fall from his pony.

After the shock of the invasion had passed, the Turks proved to be a shot in the arm for India. The Persian language spoken at court enriched Indian literature and combined with the Sanskrit-based dialects of northern India to create Hindustani. Painting and architecture were infused with life, roads were paved, and, in the 14th century, Delhi was pronounced by the Arab traveller Ibn Batuta to be the most magnificent city in the whole Muslim world. Conversion to the Islamic faith was seen as a means of advancement, and those Rajputs who didn't take advantage of this offer were able to sharpen their martial skills in constant guerrilla warfare.

The Turks adopted the Indian cuisine and costume as well as a modified form of the Hindu caste system. Highest were those of foreign extraction such as Turks, Arabs, Afghans, and Persians, known as *ashraf* (that is, "honorable"). Then came upper-caste converts from Hinduism, the "clean" castes of both merchants and artisans, and then the "unclean" occupations of scavengers.

It's worth noting that the first—and last—Muslim woman to rule in India was Qutb-ud-din's granddaughter Raziyya. "Wise, just, and generous," a contemporary Muslim historian said of her, "but she was not born of the right sex and so all the virtues were worthless." Three years of her wisdom, justice, and generosity were all they could take before they murdered her.

What they seemed to want was a despot like Ala-ud-din Khalji (1296–1316), who forced Mongol invaders back across the Afghan frontier and then moved through the peninsula to its southern tip. But Ala-ud-din's successors did not assert control of the territory. The south remained dominated by the Hindu kingdom of Vijayanagar for the next 250 years.

The Delhi sultanate under the Tughlaq dynasty could no longer hold its own in the north, and so Muslim kingdoms began to form in Bengal and the Deccan. The end was hastened by a man who made other Muslim invaders seem like pussy cats: the Mongol Timur the Lame, the "barbarous and bloody Tamburlaine," later written about by Elizabethan playwright Christopher Marlowe.

On the grounds that the sultans were too soft, he cut through Delhi in 1398, slaughtering thousands of Hindus and carrying off thousands more as slaves. He left behind him famine and pestilence. The Turks' Indian empire in splinters, it passed into the hands of Afghan horse-breeders—the Lodi—who later succumbed to his descendants, the Mughals.

Down on the Malabar coast, the great Portuguese explorer Vasco da Gama landed in 1498, paving the way for his countrymen to form a settlement in Goa. The merchants wanted to divert trade away from the Arabs, fearing the enrichment of the North African Maghreb as a threat to Christian Europe. With them came the Catholic missionaries, who found the best subjects for their teachings among the low-caste Hindus. Around 1548 St. Francis Xavier began his mission among the pearl fishermen of Goa, before he set sail for Japan. To deal with the small communities of Jews and Nestorian Christian "heretics," who had settled down on the Malabar coast in the mists of antiquity, the then Archbishop of Goa opened a local branch of the Holy Inquisition.

The merchants at first tried the soft sell, offering cloth, wine, and necklaces for ivory and gold, but the traders of Calicut were insulted at being taken for "natives" who could be bought with cheap hooch and glass baubles. The Portuguese turned to the harder sell of naval batteries, driving off a trading fleet in the year 1509 in order to control the Malabar coast. With hardly any women present in the colony, the Portuguese soldiers took Indian wives. Many Goans are descended from them or from converts who took the name of their Portuguese sponsors.

The Great Mughals

The new conquerors of northern India did not come uninvited. The Afghan governors of the Sind and the Punjab, who were hoping for more autonomy than they had under the lofty sultan Ibrahim Lodi in Delhi, therefore called on Babur the Tiger, King of Kabul.

Babur the Tiger, descendant of Timur the Lame and of Genghis Khan, accepted their welcome but made no promises. His men crushed sultan Ibrahim's 50,000 with cannons, hitherto unknown in India, at Panipat, north of Delhi.

It was the morning of 21 April 1526, the beginning of the empire of the Mughals— the term used for descendants of Babur as distinct from those of Genghis Khan, who are referred to as "Mongols" even though the terms are etymologically the same. Babur fought resistance from the Rajputs and captured Delhi and Agra, then conquered the Afghan chiefs in 1529. He died a year later.

The stately tomb of Humayun houses a ruler who lived and died under the influence of opium.

His heir, Humayun, preferred opium and astrology to complex State affairs; he was driven out of India into Persia by General Sher Shah, who proved to be a much more able ruler. In five years, the General built new roads, created a royal postal service, and set the pattern of Mughal administration for the next two centuries before dying in battle and leaving the throne to a number of inept successors and, eventually, the return of Humayun.

Straightened out for a while, Humayun came back in 1555 with his Persian army to recapture the Punjab, Delhi, and Agra, but the next year his opium habit caused his death (see page 64). He did, however, leave a son named Akbar.

The most famous—and possibly most stunning—memorial to love ever built, the Taj Mahal.

Jalal-ud-din Mohammed Akbar (1556–1605) was a real emperor. Typical of his genius was the new religion he offered his subjects: the Divine Faith (*Din-Ilahi*), intended to satisfy orthodox Muslims and those who, just like himself and the Hindus, appreciated the idea of a semi-divine ruler. Keen to win the allegiance of the Hindus, Akbar abolished most of the discriminatory taxes on non-Muslims, and recruited Rajputs for his army after marrying a daughter of Raja Bharmal of Amber, (though he did not flinch at massacring another 8,000 Rajput soldiers).

But despite repeated efforts, Akbar could not extend his empire south. In 1565, the Muslim sultanates of the Deccan had taken the Hindu empire of Vijayanagar by means of slaughter, but they were not going to hand it all to Akbar.

Although illiterate, Akbar had enormous intellectual curiosity. He preferred Sufi mysticism to orthodox Islam, and held debates with

Brahmins, Jain monks, Parsi Zoroastrians, and Jesuits. The more orthodox Muslims were concerned that Islam was being abandoned, and rebellions sprang up in Bengal, Bihar, and the Punjab.

While Akbar was fighting in the Deccan in 1601, his son claimed the throne. Akbar rushed back to reassert his power but he died soon after, poisoned, it is rumored, by his son. The new emperor called himself Jahangir (World Seizer) but once in power he left affairs of state to his wife Nur Jahan, as he was more interested in writing poetry, drinking a great deal of wine, and taking summer excursions up to Kashmir. Here, rich Persian culture dictated taste in dress, décor, manners, and morals, enriched by the Hindu culture of the Rajputs in literature, cuisine, and sexuality. If the peasants were squeezed by taxes to pay for the luxury of Mughal court life, it was a boon for the country's artisans —goldsmiths, jewelers, and weavers. In such an atmosphere, incidents of highway banditry increased and the district governors shared the rich booty in exchange for a pardon when the bandits were captured.

Jahangir's son Shahjahan became the biggest spender of all the Mughals. He lavished millions on palaces and mosques, blowing at least one million pounds sterling on gold and jewels for his Peacock Throne. Despite this, the imperial treasury allotted only 5,000 rupees a week for the plague and famine victims of 1631.

Of several hundred women in the emperor's harem, his only love was the now legendary Mumtaz-Mahal ("Exalted of the Palace"), by whom he had 14 children. She died in childbirth and Shahjahan built her the most famous memorial a man ever offered to the woman he loved: the Taj Mahal.

Shahjahan's son was Aurangzeb (1658–1707), who overthrew his father and imprisoned him in the Agra fort for the last years of his life. A pious Muslim, puritanical in both clothes and personal tastes, he banished music from the court and burned the portraits of princes as breaches of the Islamic taboo on graven images. Gone, too, was any notion of religious tolerance. The Sikhs were slaughtered, the Hindu temples in both Varanasi and Mathura were destroyed, and the building of new temples was forbidden. Taxes on non-Muslims were brought back; Hindu merchants were forced to pay double duties on their goods.

Aurangzeb streamlined the lax administration of his predecessors, but he almost bankrupted the realm with his campaigns to expand the empire down to the south, and his battles against rebels in the north. The most significant resistance came from Marathas, in today's State of Maharashtra, around Mumbai. They were led by the fighter Shivaji (1627–1680), bandit, brave military commander, and an authentic Hindu folk hero.

Starting out from Pune, Shivaji's Marathas fought off the Deccan sultans at Bijapur and the Mughals at Purandar. Aurangzeb forced him finally to submit, but the humiliating reception he was given at court sent him back on the warpath again. Shivaji then had himself crowned King of the Marathas and, to pay his soldiers, plundered the country all the way east to Madras.

The British Arrive

Meanwhile, by the middle of the 17th century, Dutch and British armed merchant ships had broken through the Portuguese blockade to set up their East India Companies on both coasts. Arriving in 1608, the British took five years to get their foot in the Indian door, at the western port of Surat, north of Bombay. The Company destroyed the Portuguese fleet and took over the protection of the Muslim pilgrimage ships to Mecca, but there were no hard feelings; the Portuguese made a gift of Bombay to King Charles II in 1661 as part of the dowry of Catherine of Braganza. The Indians were not consulted.

The Company erected its east-coast installations in the year 1642 just down the road from the Dutch, at Mandaraz, pronounced "Madras" by the British. Further north, the British gradually gained the upper hand over their rivals, now including the French, for the Bengali trade that was to create Calcutta.

The Mughal empire had five rulers in 12 years after Aurangzeb died. Bihar, Bengal, and Rajputana all went their separate ways. The

A monument to the bygone Raj, the Victoria Memorial was paid for by "voluntary contributions" from maharajas and nawabs.

Sikhs reacted violently to persecution, and the Marathas spread to Orissa, after which, in the year 1739, Nadir Shah of Persia invaded and carried off the Peacock Throne (broken up after his assassination). Meanwhile, the British clerk-turned-soldier Robert Clive won a long campaign against the French for Madras.

Fearing the Europeans would start carving up Bengal, the nawab (Muslim prince) Siraj-ud-daula set up an attack on the British settlement in Calcutta on the hot day of 20 June, 1756. Those who did not flee to sea were thrown into Fort William's prison, already known as the Black Hole. It's still being debated whether 123 suffocated and 23 survived or "only" 43 died, leaving 21 survivors, but however many died, they were enough impetus for Clive to crush Siraj-ud-daula at the Battle of Plassey. Clive became governor and placed his own nawab on the throne, in exchange for £500,000 for himself and the Company. He then annexed about 2,330 sq km (900 sq miles) of land due south of Calcutta to provide rents for the British settlement and to guarantee himself an income of £30,000 per year for life. The rise of the British Empire in India had begun.

Installing the Raj

The arrival of Indian merchants, including Jains, Parsis, and Jews, turned Bombay, Madras, and Calcutta into large cities; the Company discovered a knack for large-scale administration. A high sense of integrity took the place of what Clive called "fighting, chicanery, intrigues, politics, and Lord knows what." In return for fixed payments to the emperor, Company officials collected revenue. With a well-paid civil service, Clive's successors—Warren Hastings and Lord Cornwallis—avoided the collectors by padding their salaries with private deals. With the new title of Governor-General, Hastings and then Cornwallis were responsible to the British government rather than the Company. Britain began taking India more seriously. But this new high-mindedness had in it the seeds of future discontent. Indians were removed from key positions in the administration because Cornwallis considered them not yet up to the stricter ethical standards that were being introduced. It took a long time for them to be readmitted to positions of responsibility.

Clive's example in Calcutta set the pattern for territorial control around the country. In the south, Tipu Sultan of Mysore remained a menace to Madras until Governor-General Arthur Wellesley, future Duke of Wellington, defeated him. Wellesley then turned on the Marathas, whose clans controlled the puppet Mughal emperor in Delhi and much of central India. A few brilliant victories gained control of Orissa and other territories for Britain, but London decided all that energy would be best directed at Napoleon, and called Wellesley home.

When territory wasn't acquired by conquest—Sind from Baluchi princes, Punjab and Kashmir from the Sikhs, Maharashtra and Delhi from the Marathas, or Assam from Burma—the British annexed it by so-called Principles of Lapse and Paramountcy. If a ruler died without direct heir, his state "lapsed" into British hands. If, after repeated warnings, a State was judged guilty of misgovernment, it was simply annexed by the Paramount Power—the British.

Schools and colleges became established. Calcutta became the center of a vigorous free press and the intellectual capital of India. During 1834, regional rupees of differing value were minted with the portrait of the Mughal emperor. Then a national rupee of unitary value was issued, with the face of the king of England. In running the empire effectively, the British installed railways, better roads, the telegraph, and stamp-post. Indians also saw the other side of the Industrial Revolution as their cotton left for Manchester to come back as cloth cheaper than their own.

Men such as Governor-General William Bentinck worked with missionaries and reformers such as Brahman Ram Mohan Roy to legislate against the practice of widows becoming sati by climbing onto the funeral pyres of their respective husbands. Other campaigns were launched against female infanticide, slavery, and the bands of Thugs (devotees of Kali) ranging the countryside.

Although some Indians assimilated the language and behavior of the British, to most the imperialists were offensively aloof. The Indians had known other conquerors, but at least they had been able to gain a sense of them as human beings. The British Raj, though, was firmly entrenched in clubs, and remained resolutely separate.

Mutiny and Reform

The cause of the Mutiny of 1857, or The War of Independence as it is known to Indians, was symptomatic of British insensitivity. Indian troops were trained to bite the cartridges before loading their rifles, but some were greased with animal fat and the Indians felt they were ingesting either fat from the cow, sacred to the Hindus, or lard from the pig, abomination to the Muslims. As they had suffered slights of either incomprehension or contempt for their religious customs before, they simply could not believe it was not deliberate, and mutiny broke out at Meerut, 40 km (25 miles) north of Delhi.

The cartridge blunder became a pretext for avenging other grievances, with troops rallying around the rulers dispossessed by Lapse or Paramountcy. The mutineers then invaded Delhi, Kanpur (Cawnpore), and Lucknow, looting treasuries, breaking open jails, and killing British men, women, and children.

The British retaliated with equal savagery against the mutineers and against civilians in the country through which the relief columns passed. Finally, the last of the proud Mughals, the Emperor Bahadur Shah, was condemned to exile in Burma.

Nothing could more aptly epitomize the Mutiny's good and bad results, from an Indian point of view, than the name given to the leg-

Lucknow was an important center for Indian mutineers, who rallied here against British contempt for their sacred customs.

islation that was to follow: the 1858 Act for Better Government of India. The British evidently saw the need to improve things for the Indians, but also decided to tighten their imperial hold.

The East India Company was replaced by a Government with a Viceroy answering to a Secretary of State for India in London. The bureaucracy was to be streamlined, and the army reorganized to raise the ratio of British to Indians.

Indian education was greatly expanded, though less successfully in rural areas where people thought it better to be a good peasant than a bad clerk. Queen Victoria, who in the year 1876 would add the title Empress of India to her roll of honor, proclaimed that the Indian Civil Service would be open to "our subjects of whatever race and creed." Not a lot of Indians, however, could afford the trip to Britain to take the examination.

Meanwhile, lawyers were at a premium—Indians love litigation and it was ideal training for future politicians—and politics had been clandestine, because it was so often fatal to express an opinion on the wrong (i.e., losing) side. Now open political debate flourished, especially in Calcutta where Karl Marx was much appreciated.

Indian entrepreneurs developed their own cotton mills in Bombay, Ahmedabad, Kanpur, and Madras, but the new tea gardens were a strictly British affair. Indian agricultural products soon found new markets in Europe when the Suez Canal was opened in 1869.

In the arts, architecture was often of the work of engineers, and huge sculptures were ordered from Victorian Britain rather than from local artists. The bright spot was the Archaeological Survey of 1871 to preserve ancient monuments. British soldiers hunting tigers in the jungle were finding temples and palaces many Indians no longer knew existed.

Fighting for Self-Rule

The Indian National Congress, the country's first political party, held its inaugural meeting in Bombay in 1885. As a group of liberal Hindu and Parsi intellectuals, supported by a few progressive

British, it was more national in purpose than in its representation. Lacking connection with the peasants, it was also distrusted by conservative landlords and by most Muslims. The goal of *swaraj* (self-rule), proclaimed in 1906, was seen by a moderate Left Center group as government within the British Empire, and by a breakaway revolutionary Extreme Left group as complete independence.

After years of subservience to the West, artists returned to Indian themes in their literature, theatre, and music. Indians applauded the decision of Lord Ripon to allow Indian magistrates to try British defendants in criminal cases, but attempts at social reform such as protecting child brides against rape by their husbands were fought by traditionalist Hindus from Calcutta and Pune with cries of "religion in danger." Self assertion reigned again: After years of peace, hostilities broke out between the Hindus and the Muslims.

In Maharashtra, a cult grew up around the Maratha leader Shivaji (see page 42) against the British and also the Muslims whom Shivaji had fought all his life. Fundamentalists took to the streets to protest against the Muslim slaughter of cows. There was a movement to convert Muslims and Christians back to the "national" religion. The Muslims tried to purify the Islamic practice of the Hindu rituals which had accrued over the years.

The caste system was affected by this new spirit. Untouchables pressed for better treatment, but their cause was not helped by the activism of American missionaries and the Salvation Army, who gave other castes a good excuse to resist "foreign interference."

Dynamic Lord Curzon, viceroy from 1899 to 1905, was driven by a lofty imperial vision of the British role in India. His grandiose life in the viceregal residence in Calcutta or palace in Simla was worthy of the Mughal emperors.

Highly active in excavating and restoring the temples and palaces, Curzon also did more than any of his predecessors, adding 9,000 km (5,500 miles) of new railway lines, working to modernize farming with an agricultural research institute, and building an irrigation system that would become a model for Asia and Africa. The Indians, however, resented his refusal to consult them, and rioted over an ill-considered partition of Bengal.

In 1911, King George V became the first British monarch to visit India. He celebrated the fact by announcing that the capital would be moved from Calcutta to a whole new city to be built in Delhi. The Royal architects Edwin Lutyens and Herbert Baker created a monumental New Delhi with triumphal arches, palaces, gigantic government buildings, and sweeping avenues radiating from circles (for easy riot control)—the stuff of an empire meant to last forever.

Without giving up demands for self-determination, India fought at Britain's side in World War I, and more than one Prussian general blinked at Rajput and Sikh princes leading an Indian infantry through the trenches of France.

This monument illustrates the march to the sea that Mahatma Gandhi led in protest against the British salt tax.

In 1917 self-determination in India seemed nearer when London announced its plan for "the progressive realization of responsible government in India as an integral part of the (British) Empire." The British were not letting go, but a new Government of India Act two years later promised Indians real executive power at the head of provincial ministries for education, public works, health, and agriculture. The moderate Indians were delighted, but revolutionaries saw it as a foot in the door, while many British officials retired rather than serve under Indian ministers.

Riots over Bengal's partition led to new laws for political trials without jury and also internment without trial. Popular protest in the big cities in 1919 at first took the non-violent form of a *hartal*, an Indian "strike" called when the soul is shocked by an injustice. This idea came from the new leader Mohandas Karamchand Gandhi, dubbed *Mahatma* (Great Soul) by the Indian poet Rabindranath Tagore.

Gandhi returned in 1915 after working as a lawyer defending the rights of the Indian community in South Africa. The moral strength of his non-violent philosophy was immediately tested in the Punjab, where the hartal erupted into riots. In Amritsar, the troops of General Reginald Dyer fired on a prohibited mass meeting, leaving 379 dead and over 1,200 wounded.

As a result, Gradualist reform became discredited and civil unrest a feature of everyday life. Declaring that "cooperation in any form with this satanic government is sinful," Gandhi advocated the boycott of elections and the withdrawal of people from government office. Moderates held on, but the election boycott was at least 33 percent successful.

Abandoning European dress for his now legendary white cotton *dhoti* (loincloth) and shawl, and drawing spiritual guidance from all the great religions of India, Gandhi became the simple but powerful symbol of India. He supported the Untouchables and defended the rights of village artisans and peasants, but his non-violent movement could not stop the escalating riots among the religious communities.

Worried by the spread of his civil disobedience movement, the British jailed Gandhi in 1922 for two years. In jail at the same time, for "incitement to rebellion," was Congress Party member Jawahar-lal Nehru, who was British-educated but also a Brahman intellectual, as his honorary title of *Pandit* suggested. He was the Mahatma's favorite to lead India to independence.

Independence with Partition

The British began to see India's independence as inevitable; however, only a few seemed to understand the vital role of the religious groups. Britain prepared a parliamentary democracy with majority rule, but the majority were Hindus—and Hindus, Muslims, and Sikhs had been killing each other in war for many centuries.

Nehru's Congress Party, largely Hindu with a socialist leadership, wanted a parliamentary democracy. As counterweight, British legislation reserved parliamentary seats for religious minorities, but the Punjab and Bengal had such a complicated mixture of Hindus, Muslims, and Sikhs that it was not possible to avoid fights over how separate constituencies were to be formed. The seeds of future trouble were sown.

The legislation on reserving seats gave the Muslims the basis for an alternative to an India in which they were only a quarter of the population: Partition. In 1930, the poet Muhammad Iqbal proposed a separate Muslim homeland in the northwest of India. A small group of Indian Muslims at Cambridge came up with the name Pakistan, using the initials of the Punjab, Afghania (N.W. Frontier Province), Kashmir, and Sind (at the same time producing the word *pak*, meaning "pure"), and adding "stan," the Persian suffix for the word "country." The Muslim campaign for Partition was led by London-trained Bombay lawyer, Muhammad Ali Jinnah.

Meanwhile, Gandhi vehemently opposed any dismemberment of the country, and tried to keep people united by fasting to uphold the spirit of love, and by focussing on the common adversary: the British. Advocating civil disobedience, he led his famous Salt March to the sea, to scoop up salt and circumvent the hated British salt tax. This put more than 60,000 in jail.

The Raj Ghat, shrine to the "Great Soul" of Gandhi, sees thousands of pilgrims and supporters to this day.

Against this militancy, World War II did not elicit the solidarity of the first. Indians courageously fought alongside the British troops, in Burma, the Middle East, and Europe, but Gandhi saw the British as a provocation for Japanese invasion and was jailed yet again, for launching a "Quit India" campaign in the year 1942. Some anti-British extremists saw the Japanese as an Asian liberator.

Winston Churchill didn't want any Indian independence and so it was probably as well for India that he was defeated by Attlee's Labor Party in 1945.

With riots growing ever more bloody in Bengal, Bihar, and the Punjab, India's last viceroy, Lord Mountbatten, kept a mandate to make the British departure as quick and as smooth as possible. Quick it was—six months after his arrival—but not smooth.

Midnight, 14–15 August, in the year 1947, was a moment, in the words of Prime Minister Nehru, "when we step out from the old to

the new, when an age ends, and when the soul of a nation, long sup-
pressed, finds utterance."

Nehru got his Independence and Jinnah his Partition—a Pakistan
whose eastern Bengali portion was to break away 24 years later to
become Bangladesh. Bloodshed began as soon as the Partition
boundaries were set. In east (Indian) Punjab, Hindus and Sikhs massacred Muslims; in west (Pakistani) Punjab, the Muslims massacred
Sikhs and Hindus. This was followed by a mass exodus of millions
from one country to the other but the convoys often ended in slaughter. Delhi itself was torn apart by communal rampages. The overall
death toll came to at least 500,000 people.

Mahatma Gandhi immediately rushed from Calcutta to Delhi to
defend Muslims against further slaughter. In January 1948, he fasted
for peace in the capital city in order to force the Indian government
to pay Pakistan the monies due in the Partition's division of assets. A
Hindu fanatic, enraged by what he felt was an excessively fervent
defense of the Muslim interests, assassinated Gandhi in a prayer
meeting on 30 January.

India Today

Sensitive and sophisticated, Pandit Nehru was also the strongest ruler
India had known since the great Mughals and, like them, he created a
powerful dynasty. Rejecting his mentor Gandhi's faith in a village-
based democracy, Nehru worked to make India a fully industrialized
society on the basis of democratic socialism. Established industries
had their taxes raised but were not nationalized. Companies that were
foreign had to accept Indian financial participation and management.

He appropriated for the State much of the personal fortunes of the
princes, but found it harder to curtail the power of land-owners who
had extensive contacts with the more conservative elements in his
Congress Party.

Kashmir remained an unresolved problem of Partition. The Muslim majority in the Vale of Kashmir and Gilgit made it part of Pak-

istan, but the greater part of the eastern region around Jammu was Hindu, as was the maharaja. Backed by Pakistan, Pathan tribesmen invaded Kashmir in 1947 to force the issue, but were soon repulsed by Indian troops flown in when the maharaja hastily acceded to India. Kashmir was divided between both India and Pakistan, pending a plebiscite—which has never been held. An invasion by Pakistan in 1965 was aborted and has left the issue distinctly moot.

Applying the principle of geographical integrity, Nehru regained French Pondicherry by negotiation after Independence, and Portuguese Goa by force in 1961. He was less successful in fighting China over territory on the Tibetan frontier. Egalitarian and agnos-

tic, Nehru passed laws against the injustice of the caste system, child-marriage, and the treatment of women in Hindu households, but century-old customs die hard: before his death in 1964, he asked that his ashes be scattered in the Yamuna river at Delhi and the Ganga at Allahabad, and without ritual. The mourning crowds, though, ignored his last wishes, uttering prayers and crying: "Panditji has become immortal."

Coming to power in the year 1966 after the brief ministry of Lal Bahadur Shastri, Indira Gandhi proved strong enough in her own right for people to stop describing her as Nehru's daughter or as "not related to Mahatma Gandhi."

In fact, she learned much from both, the knack for power-politics of the one and the massive popular appeal of the other. She accelerated industrialization, in particular the nuclear power industry, including a first atomic explosion in the desert in 1974. Her proudest achievement, though, was the Green Revolution that modernized wheat and rice farming to give India, for the first time in its history, self-sufficiency in food production. Old entrenched conservatism hampered her birth-control programs to check the rocketing population growth.

Modern India looms behind the site of the age-old fishing trade in Bombay.

Indira Gandhi's tendency toward tough authoritarianism was highlighted during the repressive state of emergency she declared in 1975, describing it as "disciplined democracy," when she ordered mass arrests of opposition leaders who had charged her and her party with malpractice and corruption.

The electorate punished her in 1977 with three years in the wilderness, then brought her back with a huge majority. But her second term was beset with the problems of regional unrest, most notably in Assam in the northeastern region of the country, where local massacres left 3,000 dead, and in the Punjab, where Sikh militants staged violent demonstrations for greater autonomy and even independence. It was her order to the Indian Army in 1984 to attack armed militants in the Sikhs' sacred Golden Temple in Amritsar, resulting in 800 dead, that led to her assassination in Delhi five months later by two Sikh members of her security guards. Hindus then went on the rampage through Sikh communities, resulting in a round of communal violence.

In the spirit of his grandfather and mother, Rajiv Gandhi and the Congress party sought to improve the lot of the lower castes and minorities while modernizing India. In addition to a gas leak at the Union Carbide chemical plant that left thousands dead in Bhopal shortly after Gandhi's election to office in 1984, numerous regional conflicts at home and a somewhat schizophrenic foreign policy troubled Gandhi's term. As a result, Gandhi and his party were defeated in the elections of November 1989 by the National Front, composed of five parties including the Hindu nationalist Bharatiya Janata Party (BJP). The National Front attempted to set up a new government first with V. P. Singh and later, in 1991, with S. Chandra Shekhar as Prime Minister. The Congress Party regained power, however, following Rajiv Gandhi's assassination by a Tamil suicide bomber during election campaigns in 1991. P. V. Narasimha Rao, the new Prime Minister, adopted aggressive economic reforms to combat a looming financial crisis.

The BJP's role in provoking the 1992 demolition by Hindus of a mosque in Ayodhya, said to have been built on ground sacred to them, and the widespread racial violence which ensued caused PM Rao to ban the BJP. Though this party fell into disfavor for some time, their fundamentalist concerns, shared by members of the Shiv Sena party, increased in popularity in subsequent years. Accusations of corruption among officials in Rao's administration in 1995 also paved the way for a comeback. The BJP defeated Congress in the general elections of May 1996, winning the largest number of seats in Parliament. Represented by Prime Minister Atal Behari Vajpayee, the BJP was forced to cede its seat in less than two weeks, however, having failed in efforts to form a coalition government. The United front, composed of thirteen parties supported by Congress, placed H. D. Deve Gowda at the helm.

With the backing of Congress, PM Gowda ruled until May 1997, when Congress unseated him and appointed Inder Kurnal Gujral in his place. Despite the instability of the nation's government at this time, it is remarkable that in the year that India celebrated its 50th Anniversary of Independence, a *Dalit* (or member of an oppressed caste), K. R. Narayan, was appointed President for the first time.

In early 1998, political volatility necessitated India's first ever mid-term parliamentary elections, leading Congress to withdraw support from PM Gujral and to make Atal Behari Vajpayee of the BJP head of a multi-party coalition government. In May, Vajpayee announced the successful completion of nuclear tests, which, although touted by the Indians as a sign of their sovereignty, may complicate India's relations with its neighbors and the West.

Despite the strength of the BJP, the emergence of Rajiv Gandhi's Italian-born widow, Sonia Gandhi, as Congress Party President suggests that the legacy of the Nehru-Gandhi dynasty is far from forgotten. Their goals remain influential as India approaches the new millennium while it continues to modernize its industry and increase its agricultural output. While facing the challenges of an ever-growing population that may outnumber even that of China by the beginning of the next century, India remains the largest democracy and one of the top ten industrial powers in the world.

WHERE TO GO

Where, indeed? This subcontinent is so rich and varied that the choice of what to see on a first visit can be daunting. Don't even *think* of "doing" India the way people "do" Europe. With some judicious selection from among the places we suggest, you can most certainly get a pretty good feel for the country in the four weeks that most people devote to a first trip.

Even if you have a distinct taste for improvisation and a horror of schedules and detailed itineraries, you must accept from the outset, if your time is at all limited, that travelling around India will demand a certain amount of *planning*. Remember, there are over 844 million Indians out there, and a lot of them will be on the move at the same time as you will be, therefore competing for plane seats and hotel rooms. So you will need to make at least some advance reservations for hotels in principal cities and especially for your major plane or train journeys. This will still leave you plenty of room for getting off the beaten track and staying overnight in new and unexpected places.

Putting Together an Itinerary

We have divided the country into five regions—north, west, center, east, and south.

In each of the regions, you'll find a city such as Delhi, Mumbai, or Chennai which you can use as a starting point, and which would also be the best place for phoning home and making other practical arrangements. Equally important, each area includes a place where, in hallowed and sensible military phrasing, you can go for rest and recreation. In this case, you'll find a beach resort, nature reserve, or one of the old hill-stations of the British Raj, each being ideal for a change of pace or climate. It's easy to overdose on the many temples, palaces, and museums in India. They are all worth your attention, but do take plenty of time to relax, too—

Hand-dug irrigation channels will bring water so that this parched earth can be more successfully farmed.

you'll be surprised at how much more you can see and appreciate if you've had enough rest.

If your budget allows you to fly around the country, you can design a "smorgasbord" of places to see in each region, since you will not be able to do all of them exhaustively. In any case, we recommend that you choose from at least two of them, ideally three, when planning your "menu."

Tourist Information offices can be very helpful. You will find their guides are much more reliable than those outside the temples or palaces, but one word of warning: different tour guides will give contradictory explanations about the significance of statues as well as many different versions of legend and historical "fact." It would be easy to dismiss these explanations as being nonsense, but you'll understand India better if you can appreciate that what each guide is saying may in its own way be *true*. When it comes to ideas, there is no more tolerant land on earth.

Practical Hints

The HANDY TRAVEL TIPS section at the back of the book offers details on how to handle the practical side of your trip, but it's worth keeping a few points in mind when deciding where you're going in the time you have available.

The climate in India (see page 235) imposes its own imperatives and restrictions on your itinerary. Northern India is simply impracti-

cal in December, Delhi unbearably hot in June, and trains uncertain in the monsoon. Think of three seasons, *cool*, *hot*, and *wet*, emphasized here because they take on a particular meaning in the Indian context.

The cool season is from October to March, the ideal time for seeing most of India (except in the northern hills and mountains, where it's bitterly cold). Cool means it is pleasantly warm by day, and fresh enough for a sweater in the evening. The temperature begins to rise by mid-February. Hot, from April

Vestiges of the old Mughal empire at Agra, as seen from the Lal Quila, or Red Fort.

to June, is hot as people only rarely experience it. The cities and plains in this season are definitely a bad bet, but the hill-stations will be at their best. From mid-June to September, wet means monsoon-wet, not all day every day, but torrential rains occur often enough to make travel uncertain and the mosquitoes and other bugs a real nuisance. However, during this time the country is at its most green, and the monuments, especially the Taj Mahal, take on a glistening beauty.

With regard to your health (see also page 241), two attitudes herald a miserable time: carelessness and hypochondria. Take elementary precautions by sticking to bottled drinks and freshly cooked food, and you won't have any serious stomach problems. An occasional touch of "Delhi belly" is unavoidable when you're not used to the spicy food, but nothing to worry about; take it easy and drink lots of liquids, and it'll pass. If you are on a short trip, you may need to take a quick-acting remedy to keep you on your feet, but if you load up with antibiotics and a host of other patent medicines, your body will never build up resistance, and the next attack will just be worse.

There is one essential: protect yourself from the heat. Save your sun-tanning for the beach or the hotel swimming pool. Otherwise, stay out of the sun. Wear a nicely ventilated hat and keep to the shade in the street. Try to do your open air sightseeing in the morning and

Like a Maharaja

From the beginning of October to the end of March, Indian Railways organize one-week tours of Rajasthan (plus Agra and Delhi) on a train they call Palace on Wheels, reproducing the luxury once enjoyed only by maharajas.

The train takes you from Delhi on to Jaipur, Udaipur, Jaisalmer, Jodhpur, Bharatpur, Agra, and back to Delhi, with boat cruises and rides on camels and proud elephants along the way. Book in advance from your travel agency before you leave home. It's not cheap, but then, that's what makes you feel like a maharaja.

*It is possible to visit the fort at Agra in style by taking a ride
in this palace on wheels.*

late afternoon. Take a siesta after lunch. Drink plenty of liquids—in
the heat, dehydration is more of a risk than an upset stomach.

In all senses of the word, stay cool. In the first few days jet-lag,
acclimatization, and culture shock may lead you to lose your temper
when you see the airports, railways, and hotels not organized in a
way you're used to, but don't forget—John Kenneth Galbraith
called it a *functioning* anarchy. Count to ten, and, like Delhi belly,
it'll pass. Airports, railway stations, and hotels can be a pain anywhere in the world these days. Indians are mostly cheerful, respond-
ing much more readily to a smile than a scowl.

The red tape can at times seem like barbed wire, but this, too, can be handled. Part of India's legacy after several centuries of bureaucracy (don't just blame the British civil service—it began long before) is an inordinate respect for the written document and the rubber stamp. Don't knock it—use it. Vouchers, passes, letters of introduction, and printed business cards all work like magic when a "confirmed" reservation has become "unconfirmed."

If you should be travelling by train (see page 253) and rate comfort above improvisation, go first class with an *Indrail Pass*. It saves you time in queues and gets you preferential treatment with reservations. Indian Airlines' *Discover India* plan offers 21 days of unlimited travel and is less economic than single tickets, but buy them *en bloc* with confirmed reservations that you should reconfirm at each new airport.

Echoing around every office you will hear the cheerful sentence: "No problem." Though it rarely means exactly this, interpret it as meaning "no catastrophe" and have a good time anyway.

THE NORTH

The region around Delhi embraces the government capital—the heart of the old Mughal empire at Agra, and the nature reserves of

Corbett and Bharatpur. In the Himalayan mountains there is the hill-station of Simla —which once served as the British summer capital—and the magical but dangerous region of Kashmir.

Delhi

On the Yamuna (Jumna) river at the western end of the great Ganga valley, the capital seems to have been a coveted place for India's conquerors. Though they each very often destroyed the work of their predecessors, the 20th-century city remains a fascinating compendium of India's imperial history.

Recent archaeological findings suggest that a site on the Yamuna river may have been the home of *Mahabharata* hero, Yudhishthira, dating back to 1000 B.C. A rock inscription from Emperor Ashoka indicates that Delhi was a major point on the trade route between the northwest frontier and Bengal in the third century B.C.

The Tomara Rajputs made it their capital in 736, with the name of Dhillika, and it was a focus of clan wars until the Muslims conquered it and Qutb-ud-din Aybak set up his sultanate in 1206. Delhi was dismantled to make way for new monuments which then suffered from the devastating passage of Timur the Lame in 1398. He took away 90 elephant-loads of building materials and thousands of skilled Delhi stonemasons and sculptors to build his mosque at Samarkand. With the advent of the Mughals in 1526, Delhi alternated with Agra as the capital, and each ruler asserted his particular taste in architectural caprice.

Under the British, the town took a back seat to the ports of Calcutta, Bombay, and Madras until 1911, when it became once more a proud imperial capital. No less vain than the Mughals, the new conquerors all added their own architectural tastes, which were a tribute to India's past but unmistakably British in overall conception, to New Delhi.

Stone Cold Stoned

Everybody thought that Emperor Humayun had kicked his opium addiction when he returned from exile in Persia to reclaim his throne in 1555. But one day in the Sher-Mandal, which he had converted into a place where he could study his books on astrology and secretly indulge his habit, he was coming down the stairs, feeling more than a little woozy, when the muezzin at the local mosque started calling the faithful to prayer. Legend has it that the Great Mughal tried to kneel right there on the staircase, tumbling over and fatally cracking his head.

The looming specter of India Gate offers a proud but rather hazy reminder of the time of the British Raj.

Today, a tour of the capital takes you through a mixture of imposing ministries and embassies, modern office buildings and hotels, and along the Old Delhi of vibrant Hindu and Muslim communities crowding in on the Mughal monuments. For more orientation, visit the Tourist Information Office on Janpath.

Delhi of the Sultans

Start at the southern end of the city, with the **Qutb Minar**, a symbol of Islam's impact on India. Begun by Delhi's first sultan, Qutb-ud-din, and completed by his son-in-law Iltutmish, the 73-m (240-ft) tower was erected to celebrate the Turkish conquest of Delhi. The tower comprises four stories, each a tapering cylinder with angular and convex ribs, separated by balconies.

The top of the tower is off limits, due to dangers inherent in the narrow staircase that leads to the look-out point, so the best bet for a panoramic view of the city is the top floor of one of the taller, more recent hotels.

The ruins of the ancient mosque **Quwwatu'l-Islam-Masjid** (which means "The Might of Islam"), was built with the might of the Hindus. With no skilled Muslim labor at his disposal, Qutb called on local craftsmen to build the mosque from the ruins of 27 Hindu and Jain temples, demolished by their own elephants. You can see the re-

sults of this construction method in the temple-pillars set on top of one another. Sculptures have been plastered over, but the Indian carving remains. Islamic architecture shows in the five characteristic peaked arches of the prayer-hall screen, but even here the decoration, which includes the Arabic lettering, is naturalistic and Hindu in style.

In the mosque's courtyard, there is a 7-m (22-ft) **Iron Pillar**, from the fourth century, brought here by the Rajput founders of Dhillika, but nobody knows from where. Without rust after 1600 years worth of monsoon, this monument to the Hindu god Vishnu is said to have special properties: if you stand with your back against it and completely encircle it with your arms—no mean feat—good luck is yours for the rest of the day.

City of the Mughals

Due east of New Delhi's India Gate the much-plundered 16th-century **Purana Qila** (Old Fort) stands on an ancient mound, now believed to mark the site of Indraprastha of the *Mahabharata* epic.

The earliest Mughal building, the **Qal'a-i-Kuhna-Masjid**, with its minutely detailed molding of graceful peaked arches, represents an important transition from the Turco-Afghan to the

Protesters at the Lal Quila no longer need worry about dying under elephants' feet.

Tattoos painted on with henna for festive occasions are highly decorative, but not indelible.

sophisticated style of the Persian-influenced Mughals. The mosque was built in the year 1541 by Sher Shah, the Emperor Babur's General in office. **Sher-Mandal**, the octagonal tower due south of the mosque, served as the General's pleasure-palace, but it was to be the death of his rival and successor, Humayun (see page 39).

From Humayun's death came the splendid monument located in Nizamuddin, the **Tomb of Humayun**, which was built by his widow Haji Begum and the inspiration for the Taj Mahal. It is set back on a raised terrace in a set of walled-in tree-shaded lawns surrounded by hedges, but without the water once running in its channels ("rivers of life"), or the rectangular pools that were to be the perfect setting for the Taj. Humayun's Tomb has a remarkable charm of its own, a site for repose and serenity made from a delicate combination of materials—buff-and-red sandstone and smart, grey-trimmed white marble. With a majestic dome uniting the four octagonal kiosks over the terrace's latticed arches, this is the first fully-realized master-piece of Mughal architecture. The numerous six-pointed stars set in the abutments of the main arches are not the Jewish Star of David but an esoteric emblem that you'll see all over the country.

Dominating Old Delhi, the **Lal Quila** (Red Fort) was built by Shahjahan when he transferred the capital back to Delhi from Agra. Behind its ramparts, the Delhi citadel is more a palace than a fortress, with white marble preferred over the region's red sandstone. It's thought he used the same architect who worked on the Taj Mahal.

From south of the Fort, notice the two monumental elephants out-side the Delhi Gate. Part of the original design, they were destroyed by Emperor Aurangzeb, who refused images susceptible to idolatry. Viceroy Lord Curzon had these replicas installed in 1903. Enter the fort on its west side at the Lahore Gate, and you find yourself in a vaulted bazaar street, an idea Shahjahan borrowed from Baghdad. Imagine administrators and Rajput princes riding on elephants

Victorian Vandals

Mongols and Persians weren't the only plunderers to vandal-ize Delhi. Most of the Red Fort's palace apartments were dis-mantled by the British to build army barracks after recapturing the city from the mutineers in 1857. This official-ly sanctioned vandalism has to be understood within the context of the vindictive climate that reigned after the mutiny. Some of the more enlightened viceroys did their best to make amends in order to protect and restore India's patrimo-ny. But Lord Curzon and other company officials often had to contend with philistine circuit judges, who thought noth-ing of whitewashing or plastering over frescoes in a Mughal mausoleum while turning it into a rest house.

The Jama Masjid, or "Friday Mosque," was the first of the open courtyard-style mosques that would be built in all Mughal cities.

through the arcade as far as the **Naqqar Khana** (Drum House), where the imperial band played and visitors were obliged to dismount.

Pass with the ghosts of these nobles and commoners through the drum house to the **Diwan-i-Am** (Hall of Public Audience). Here, under a baldaquin with 40 pillars, the Emperor sat cross-legged on his throne, the "Seat of the Shadow of God." He held audience, surrounded by nobles, at midday, while common petitioners attended in the courtyard below. As a visitor, you can admire the inlaid stone panels of birds and flowers at the back of the hall.

Entrance to the **Diwan-i-Khas** (Hall of Private Audience) was for the privileged, by ticket only. You'll find it on the left, among the palace apartments on the Yamuna river. Beautiful as it is, with carved designs on the marble columns and cusped arches, imagine it in its full glory before the ravages of Nadir Shah in 1739. His Persian troops chipped the gold out of its pillars and inlay off the ceiling, and then carted away the fabulous Peacock Throne. Above the arches you'll see the inscription:

> "If paradise on earth there be,
> 'Tis here, 'tis here, 'tis here!"

The last emperor to enjoy it was King George V, for whom a painted wooden ceiling was installed.

One of the few surviving palace apartments is the principal harem, **Rang Mahal** (Palace of Color). The walls' paintings have gone and water no longer flows in its indoor Nahr-i-Bihisht (River of Paradise), but mosaics made of mirrors ornament the ceiling and walls of six boudoirs, making a galaxy of stars when candle-lit (strike a match). Southernmost of the palace buildings, **Mumtaz Mahal** was part of the imperial harem and is now a small museum of Mughal artwork.

To the northwest of the Diwan-i-Khas, the **Moti Masjid** (Pearl Mosque) is the one contribution to the Fort by Shahjahan's successor, Aurangzeb. Each evening, a sound and light show at the Red Fort tells its story; details can be obtained from the Tourist Information Bureau.

Chandni Chowk, the road from the Fort's Lahore Gate, was once an avenue for processions. Today, it is the main thoroughfare linking Delhi's bazaars, which sell jewelry, clothes, and traditional sweetmeats.

On an outcrop of rock southwest of the Red Fort, Shahjahan's other great construction, the **Jama Masjid** (the great congregational "Friday Mosque"), is the largest mosque in India. The inadvisability of a morning or late afternoon visit on hot days will become apparent when you see the three pyramidal flights of stairs to the gatehouses. The 100-sq-m (1,076-sq-ft) courtyard is enclosed by long colonnades with a pavilion at each corner. The prayer hall highlights the emperor's aesthetic, in the lotus calyx on the gateway's two lantern shafts, the delicately flaring balconies on the minarets, and the stripes to emphasize the bulbous marble domes.

Raj Ghat, the simple memorial to Mahatma Gandhi overlooking the Yamuna river, is far in spirit from the Mughals but an integral part of Old Delhi. On lawns planted with trees donated by visiting heads of state, a square of marble marks the place where Gandhi was cremated. The platform has an inscription recording his last words, *Hé Ram* (Oh, God), and nearby, a sign declares that most famous Gandhi talisman: "Recall the face of the poorest and most helpless man whom you may have seen and ask yourself if the step you con-

The Bahai Temple in New Delhi boasts fine gardens perfect for a relaxing stroll.

template is going to be of any help to him." There is also a museum recording the highlights of Gandhi's life.

New Delhi

Those nostalgic for the British Empire please note: Clive Road has been named Tyagraja, Queen Victoria Road has become Rajendra Prasad, and Curzon is Kasturba Gandhi. Though the statues of British leaders have also disappeared, the British spirit remains in the city's planning. Faithful to the policy of separating the British cantonment from the Indian quarters with a railway as the barrier, the new city built for the Empire's Indian seat of government is separated from Old Delhi by the line running from Amritsar to Agra. British Neo-Classic architecture here is mixed with elements of Buddhist, Hindu, and Mughal past, and the geometry of its plan exudes the self-confidence of the Empire. As a visiting statesman once said of it: "What splendid ruins it will make!"

The commercial pivot of New Delhi is the circular arcade and bustling roundabout of **Connaught Place**. With cinemas, banks, travel agencies, restaurants, and the better craft emporiums, it's a place whose new name, Indira Chowk, does not seem to catch on. Connaught Place straddles the northeast–southwest axis which links the Jama Masjid mosque of Old Delhi to India's parliament, **Sansad Bhavan**. Designed by the famous Herbert Baker, the rather too massive, colonnaded rotunda of the parliament building is at its best illuminated at night.

The Viceroy's Residence, now the President's house, **Rashtrapati Bhavan** has wings radiating from the great grey-blue dome of the central block and the tranquil pools and lawns of its gardens, and so bespeaks the grandeur of Britain's heyday. It looms from an artificial hill along the processional avenue, Rajpath (once Kingsway), which is flanked by parklands, where India holds its marches on Republic Day, 26 January. At the other end of Rajpath stands **India Gate**, the war memorial designed by Lutyens in the style of a triumphal arch that pays tribute to 90,000 Indian Army soldiers who died in World War I.

The **Jantar Mantar**, set south of Connaught Place, is perhaps the strangest monument in New Delhi. It is difficult to believe that these bizarre shapes, staircases going nowhere, and windows in walls without rooms were built in 1724 by a serious student, rather than in the last century by some deranged architect. It is in fact the astrologico—that is, the astronomical observatory—of Rajput prince Jai Singh II from Jaipur (see page 100). Its centerpiece is the right-angled triangle, Samrat Yantra (the Supreme Instrument), with a dome acting as a sun-dial, "accurate to half a second." In addition to this structure, he built four more—in Ujjain, Varanasi, Mathura, and his native Jaipur.

Near here, surely the liveliest Hindu temple of all, **Hanuman Mandir** (Temple of the Monkey God) is a theatre where you can witness the joyous atmosphere of popular Hinduism. Hanuman is a beneficent deity predating classical Hinduism, and the reason why no one would dream of harming the little lemurs (monkeys) running around here.

Getting There—and Back

Unless it's unavoidable, don't try to do Agra in one day. It's possible (and certainly better than missing it entirely), but it means you won't see much more than the Taj and, say, the Fort. More important, you might miss the unique beauty of the Taj as it changes in the light of different times of day.

If you are in a hurry, there's a flight from Delhi, but the comfort of an air-conditioned first-class seat on the Taj Express (3 hours) makes for an equally pleasant introduction to the big adventure of Indian railways. If you travel by car, avoid returning to Delhi after dark: the commercial traffic of goats and cows without any headlights is a notable risk for even a disciplined driver.

Alternatively, Agra is just one stop on the Indian Railways' most luxurious train, the aptly named "Palace on Wheels" (see page 61).

Museums

In what is artistically a predominantly Mughal city, the **National Museum**, on Janpath (Queensway) just south of Rajpath, is worth a visit for its collection of old Hindu sculpture, in particular those from medieval India of the kingdom of Vijayanagar.

Railway buffs will surely enjoy the display of the country's early steam engines at the open air **Rail Transport Museum**. It is situated in the diplomatic neighborhood of Chanakyapuri (behind the Bhutan Embassy). Adventurous as rail travel in India still is today, one exhibit belongs hopefully in the past: the skull of an elephant that nearly derailed a mail train in 1894.

Nehru Memorial Museum is devoted to Independence and the life of India's first Prime Minister. It is located in the house which Nehru inherited from the British Indian Army Commander-in-Chief on Teen Murti Road (it also houses a planetarium).

Agra

Location of the Taj Mahal, Agra is the most popular sight in India. Even if the place had nothing else, it would be worth the trip, for the Taj, as one calls it affectionately, is a "sight" that awakens the wonder and enthusiasm of the most blasé, world-weary traveller.

But there's plenty more. Agra was the capital of Akbar the Great, the site of his fort, of his tomb outside the city at Sikandra, and, several miles west at Fatehpur Sikri, of the marvellous deserted town he built to celebrate the birth of a son and which he abandoned to fight on the northwest frontier. Heirs of the craftsmen originally brought here continue a tradition in jewelry, brassware, ivory, and inlaid marble.

The first historical mention of Agra is in 1501, when Sultan Sikandar Lodi made it his capital. Babur captured it along with the Koh-i-Nur diamond now in the British crown jewels. His grandson Akbar chose Agra for his capital over Delhi. In the 17th century, Jahangir made it a major focus of the Islamic world. His son Shahjahan lost his taste for Agra after finishing the Taj Mahal for his wife Mumtaz-Mahal after she had died. He moved the capital back to Delhi again in 1648, leaving the city's treasure to vandals (including the British) after the 1857 Mutiny, until the viceroys organized its restoration. Today it is the effects of pollution that are taking their toll on Agra's monuments.

Taj Mahal

This is truly a monument for all seasons. There are those who swear by the sight on the Taj Mahal in the *Sharad Purnima*, the first full moon after the monsoons, a cloudless midnight in October when the light is at its clearest and also most romantic. Others love to see it in the middle of the heaviest monsoon, its marble translucent, its image blurred in the rain-stippled water channels of its gardens. But its magic is strong at any time of year, and any moment of the day. At dawn, its color changes from milk to silver to rose-pink, and at sunset it is golden. Observe it, too, in the brilliance of midday, for then it is utterly, dazzlingly *white*. On nights with a full moon, the grounds stay open till midnight.

The luminous Taj Mahal shows its many lovely colors depending on the weather and the time of day.

The **gateway** to the gardens of the mausoleum can be admired as a masterpiece in its own right, with noble marble arches, the domed kiosks on the four corner turrets, and two rows of 11 small *chhattri* (umbrella-domes) just above the entrance. It provides visitors with the perfect frame for a first view of the ensemble. You will find that long-range photography is allowed, but it is forbidden to take pictures inside the monument.

The *chharbagh* (foursquare) **gardens** are an integral part of the Taj Mahal, both spiritually, as the symbol of the paradise to which Mumtaz-Mahal has ascended, and artistically, to enhance the color and texture of the mausoleum. The dark cypresses heighten the brilliance of the monument's marble, and the water channels, meeting at a broad central viewing platform, not only provide a perfect second image, but also, with the reflection of the sky, add at dawn and sunset a subtle illumination from below.

Exquisite harmony and refined symmetry are the keynotes of the **mausoleum** itself. The structure is clad in miraculously white marble from the Rajasthan quarries of Makrana, achieving a magnificent texture with the subtly alternating broad and narrow slabs. Standing protectively at the four corners of the raised terrace, the minarets are, deferentially, slightly lower than the sublime central cupola. Inside,

A Marble Requiem

Mahal means palace, but in this case Taj Mahal is a diminutive of the name Mumtaz-Mahal (Exalted of the Palace) which Shahjahan's cousin was given when she married him. Daughter of his mother's brother, she had been his constant companion long before he succeeded to the throne and was later first lady among the hundreds in his harem. In 19 years of marriage, she bore him 14 children, dying with the birth of the last, in 1631.

Legend has it that Shahjahan's beard—he was 39, one year older than his wife— turned white practically overnight when she died, and he continued to mourn for years, dressing in white on each anniversary of her death. The 12 years taken to build her mausoleum, working untiringly with his Persian architect and with craftsmen brought from Baghdad, Italy, and France, may be regarded as the supreme sublimation of his grief. "Empire has no sweetness for me now," he wrote. "Life itself has lost all relish."

the octagonal cenotaph-chamber contains the ceremonial marble coffins of Mumtaz-Mahal and also Shahjahan, while, as was the custom of that time, the actual bodies are entombed in another chamber directly below. You'll need to light a candle or use a flashlight in the cenotaph-chamber because daylight barely filters through the beautiful marble trellis-screens.

Sadly, vandals removed all the tomb's spectacular treasures, but they did leave the gentle beauty of roses and poppies in rich inlaid stones of onyx, green chrysolite, carnelian, and variegated agate. The mausoleum is flanked by two almost identical red buildings, to the west a mosque, to the east a guest pavilion—each is a perfect viewing-point. Try the pavilion at sunrise and the mosque at sunset. But go around the back of the Taj, too, to the terrace which overlooks the Yamuna river. This boasts a view as far as the Agra Fort.

The Agra Fort

Built by Akbar in 1565, a more embattled period than during Shahjahan's construction of the Red Fort in Delhi, the Agra Fort was conceived as a citadel with a moat on three sides and a river on the fourth. Pleasure palaces were a secondary consideration, and were in fact mostly additions by Akbar's successors.

The entrance from the south, at Amar Singh Gate, takes you up a ridged elephant's ramp, sloped to slow down any potential attackers. Pass into the long quadrangle of the pillared **Diwan-i-Am** (Hall of Public Audience). It was here that Captain William Hawkins handed Emperor Jahangir a special letter of introduction from King James I. Due north is Shahjahan's **Moti Masjid** (Pearl Mosque). Climb the narrow staircase to the roof of the mosque for a fine view of the fort.

Just off the northeast corner of the Diwan-i-Am, the harem had its very own mosque, **Nagina Masjid**, Hindu temple, and between the two a bazaar where merchants sold silks and jewels. Near the *hammam* (baths), the **Diwan-i-Khas** (Hall of Private Audience) has rich carving and inlaid marble. The crack in the marble throne

While Akbar's people have long since deserted his capital, merchants here still do good business.

came from a British cannonball in 1857. As in Delhi's Fort, most of the private palace apartments face the Yamuna river. Among the most charming are the arcaded loggia and the gilt-roofed pavilions of the **Khas Mahal** or Private Palace. A minute staircase led to the **Musamman Burj**, the pavilion of the emperor's chief wife. It is also popularly known as the "Prisoner's Tower" for Aurangzeb imprisoned his father Shahjahan here, allowing him a view of his Taj Mahal.

The **Palace of Jahangir** is built around a square court with arches. There are Hindu motifs on the ceiling in the main hall, and in one on the west side: peacocks holding snakes in their beaks, for example.

Other Sights

On the river bank opposite the fort is the **Tomb of Itimad-ud-Daulah**, overshadowed by the Taj Mahal. This was built 15 years earlier by Jahangir's wife, Nur Jahan, for her father, who served as Mughal Prime Minister. There's a fragile elegance to the white marble pavilion's graceful silhouette, with a cupola and four octagonal turrets, and topped by domed kiosks. The fine lattice-work on the arches and windows is superb, but its outstanding feature is the marble inlay, which is even more abundant than in the Taj and better preserved.

Akbar's mausoleum, located at **Sikandra**, is 10 km (6 miles) north of Agra. The best view is from the top of the gateway. On the cenotaph are the 99 names of Allah.

Where Did You Go, Akbar?

The rise and fall of Fatehpur Sikri is the perfect illustration of Akbar's impulsive personality. At the end of 1568, the emperor was 26 and still without a male heir. At Sikri he met a Sufi mystic, Shaikh Salim Chishti, who promised him, given the proper spiritual dedication, not one, but three sons.

"In return for your friendship and grace," said the emperor, "I'll protect and preserve you."

Unmoved, the Sufi replied: "You can name your first son after me."

The following August, a boy was born. He was duly named Salim (later Jahangir). Overjoyed, Akbar decided to move his capital to Sikri, then embarked on a successful military campaign and came back to add the name of Fatehpur (City of Victory).

By 1581 he had abandoned Fatehpur. Only the family of Shaikh Salim Chishti remained, near the shrine Akbar had built for them. Today, 16 generations later, they're still here, but there is no sign of Akbar's people.

Fatehpur Sikri

In a country of crowded cities, it makes a refreshing change to travel 37 km (22 miles) southwest to an outcrop on which stands the citadel of Fatehpur Sikri, briefly Akbar's imperial capital.

Fatehpur, planned as a capital with Agra as a fallback position in case of attack, is protected on three sides by ramparts measuring about 6 km (4 miles). On the fourth side is an artificial lake stretching 8 km (5 miles) to the Rajasthan border, never sufficient, apparently, for the needs of the citadel, and so one of the probable reasons why Akbar did not settle here permanently.

Built by the architects working on the Agra Fort, the citadel adds the darker red stone of the mountain ridge to the usual pink sandstone.

Entering via the **Agra Gate**, at the northeast corner, one passes on the right the *karkhanas* (workshops) where carpenters, weavers, and stonemasons worked.

In the **Diwan Khana-i-Am**, the courtyard used for public audiences, Akbar dispensed his justice while attended by an executioner with instruments of torture and death. The sight of the two of them was felt to be an effective means of getting at the truth. At the foot of the colonnade is a big stone tethering-ring for an elephant whose job it was to crush capital criminals to death.

Go through the pavilion to the **Daulat Khana** (Abode of Fortune) on the south side of the courtyard, a palace of which the most striking feature is the Hindu nature of its decoration: carved pedestals with stylized elephant heads as capitals and sculpted stone screens.

In the southeast corner of the courtyard is the **Turkish Sultana's House**, or Hujra-i-Anup Talao (the Chamber of the Peerless Pool); animals covering every wall panel and pillar create the illusion of woodwork rather than stone. Fatehpur is the subject of many colorful stories in which it isn't possible to establish a historian's "truth." For instance, in the center of the courtyard is the **Pachisi Court**, a huge chessboard for the game of *pachisi*, where Akbar and his

It's said that all cats have nine lives — but since you have only one, it's best to view this creature at Corbett Park from a distance.

friends are said to have used human "pieces"— each player using a team of four slave-girls in different costumes.

Also, Akbar is said to have come to the **Astrologer's Pavilion**, in the northwest corner of the court, for a daily dose of forecasts from the house-esoteric. The emperor is known to have consulted a whole panel of experts from Hindu and Muslim schools of astrology. Just behind this is the **Treasury Pavilion**, where you can imagine Akbar seated on cushions under the arches and counting the imperial money. The pavilion was known as Ankh Michauli (Blind Man's Buff), because it was where Akbar was thought to have played "hide-and-seek" with his wives.

The purpose of the **Diwan-i-Khas** is hotly disputed; it is not necessarily the hall of private audience that its name implies. It is dominated by a great central pillar supporting bridges to a balcony. Some claim it was here that Akbar held his famous debates with Jesuits, Brahmins, Parsi Zoroastrians, Sufi mystics, Jain, and Buddhist monks —the sages arguing while Akbar sat listening atop his pillar, or Akbar striding majestically around the bridges and balcony hurling his questions at his listeners. Others insist that it was just a storehouse for jewels. Truth in India, even more than beauty, is in the eye of the beholder.

Walk across the courtyard to the beautiful five-tiered **Panch Mahal**, a palace with the Persian system of ventilation known as *badgir* (wind tower): without walls on three sides, it is open for the breezes to sweep in. Each floor is supported on columns diminishing from 84 at ground-level to four on the roof. Notice that no two columns on the ground floor are alike. Be careful on the steep climb to the top, but you'll find it is well worth it for the wonderful **view** across the citadel, particularly the palaces of the imperial harem to the southwest.

The harem's principal residence is **Jodh Bai's Palace**—built for Akbar's Hindu wife, the first royal spouse not required to convert to her husband's Islamic faith—and was Akbar's favorite residence at Fatehpur. It has one side screening out the summer heat while the other is open to the cooler breezes. Its most cherished feature is the turquoise ceramic tiled roof in the north and south wings.

Fatehpur's **Jama Masjid** (the Friday Mosque), at the south end of the citadel up on its mountain-ridge, was the very first of the open courtyard-style mosques to became characteristic of all Mughal cities. Notice the carved central *mihrab* (the recess marking the direction of Mecca). The jewel of the red stone courtyard, however, is the marble-clad **Tomb of Shaikh Salim Chishti**. Its façade features black calligraphy; in the cenotaph-chamber there are pretty painted flowers. Originally a more simple monument, its white marble "skin" was the addition of a very grateful Jahangir who, without the mystic Shaikh Salim Chishti, might never have seen the light of day.

Bharatpur

Strictly speaking, Bharatpur is in Rajasthan, but proximity, just 42 km (26 miles) due west of Agra, makes it logical to include here. The marshes of the bird sanctuary of **Keoladeo-Ghana** offer a welcome change of pace. Even if you're not an avid bird-watcher, you'll enjoy the gentle walks in the woodland, with the chance of seeing exciting herds of nilghai antelope, blackbuck, and cheetal (spotted deer). A good time to visit is just at the end of the monsoon in October—when you can see flocks of storks, egrets, and cormorants—and it is ideally combined with a full-moon trip to the Taj, but there's plenty to see all year round.

Among the more than 300 different species of birds here, you'll find eagles, cranes, pelicans, snakebirds, kingfishers, and a

Harems, the Cold Facts

The Indian Muslims' system of purdah that strictly confined women to a life behind a screen in special apartments derived from the old Persian institution of the harem. No men were allowed in the vicinity of the harem. Armed security guards inside the harem were all female, except for eunuchs who were placed at the outside doors.

In Akbar's time, women were admitted to the harem as an honor to their families, an imperial favor to some politically useful noble, certainly not always nor even very often for the emperor's sexual pleasure. Though he might have had several hundred wives, very few were his regular companions.

The senior wife, mistress of the household, was a person of great influence in the realm, guardian of one of the two imperial seals needed to authorize a new statute, and the emperor's confidante in many of his decisions. The most famous example was Mumtaz-Mahal, wife of Shahjahan, but Jahangir's wife, Nur Jahan, was much more powerful; she practically ran the whole country.

Travelers in the Punjab can find respite from their wearying journey with a short rest and a few hits from the pipe.

host of ducks and geese, as well as a flock of rare wintering Siberian cranes between January and March. The Maharaja of Bharatpur used to organize formal annual duck-shoots here for British viceroys and other top officials as well as for fellow princes. But today hunting is strictly banned. In other words, Bharatpur is only for the birds.

Corbett Park

Among India's nature reserves, this is the best known because of Jim Corbett, the audacious hunter of the man-eating tigers of Kumaon. The park was established in 1935 and was given Corbett's name after India became independent.

Northeast of Delhi, this lovely park of forest and meadows by the Ramganga river in the foothills of the Himalayas remains a home to the tiger, leopard, and elephant, as well as cheetah, sloth bear, wild pig, jackal, and hyena. The river abounds with mahseer and trout, as well as two kinds of crocodile and the occasional blind freshwater dolphin. Bird-watchers should look out for stork, red jungle-fowl, and black partridge.

The forest is thick with sissoo and tall sal trees; their timber is prized for ship-building. An elephant-ride, which allows you to swing through the jungle and grassland while reclining on a cushioned *howdah*, is a great joy. Rest at midday in the lodge at Dhikala and watch the elephants head down to the river.

Be sure to plan ahead through the Tourist Information Office or a Delhi travel agency, because admission to the park is by permit only. Permits are easy to obtain, however, and reserved accommodation can be booked either in the lodges or in the official campgrounds

Chandigarh

The capital of the Punjab is just a stopover en route to Simla, or a half-way point en route to Kashmir. It's well worth visiting this city, which was planned in 1950 by Swiss-French architect Le Corbusier, invited by the Indian government to create a new city for the post-Partition Punjab on a windy plain at the foot of the Himalayas. With British associate Maxwell Fry designing most of the housing, Le Corbusier created the leading public buildings and laid out a town of spacious boulevards and sweeping tree-lined avenues, inspired at least in part by Lutyens' ideas for New Delhi, and blessedly uncongested by growing traffic. He planned the town on the principle of the human body, with the government buildings of the **Capitol** and university at its head, the commercial town-center at its heart, and the outlying industrial districts as its limbs.

In the **Assembly** building for parliament, the **Secretariat** administrative block, the vaulted **High Court**, and the smaller **Governor's Residence**, you can see huge slabs of concrete like weathered granite from the nearby mountains. The buildings boast both geometric and amorphous shapes, with bright colors visible behind the sub-breaker grills. Take a walk through the nearby **Rock Garden** of large concrete blocks, or, to the east, take a rowboat on the artificial **Sukhna Lake**.

Most people visit the holy city of **Amritsar** for its Golden Temple Sikh Shrine. Sikh architecture may also be appreciated at the nearby Durgiana Temple. Jallianwala Bagh is an important

Highjinks in the Hills

The British established hill-stations wherever they could find a suitable area at a reasonably accessible altitude: for Chennai, Ootacamund (Ooty) in the Nilgiri Hills; for Mumbai, Mahabaleshwar in the Western Ghats; and for Delhi and Calcutta, there was a choice in the Himalayas of Simla, Mussoorie, Darjeeling, and many more. In the general relief at escaping the hell of the summer heat, they managed, in the classical British manner, to be very proper on the surface and nicely naughty underneath.

In these last bastions of the British Raj, class inevitably reared its head; each of the hill-stations, like seaside resorts back home, had their own cachet. Senior officers made so-called poodle-faking stations off limits to subalterns, who were not permitted to watch their superiors poodle-faking with other men's wives. For, as Rudyard Kipling put it:

> Jack's own Jill go up the hill
> To Muree or Chakrata.
> Jack remains and dies in the plains
> And Jill remarries soon after.

These modern tapestries in Chandigarh are a small part of the harmonious cityscape planned and executed by Le Corbusier.

monument to hundreds of martyrs who dies in an Amritsar massacre in 1919.

Simla

Similar to Chandigarh, this town, which is now capital of Himachal Pradesh, was built back in the early years of the 19th century when the British colonial settlers were desperately searching for refuge from the heat of the plains.

At an altitude of 2,130 m (6,755 ft), this was once the place where a religious ascetic offered cool spring water to the numerous weary and thirsty travelers coming out of the Himalayas. Some of these trekkers were British troops returning from the war with the Gurkhas of Nepal in 1819. They came back to build mountain retreats, as well as regular little cottages or perhaps an occasional mansion. From 1832 onwards, when governor-general Lord William Bentinck spent a happy summer here, it became the most prestigious hill-station. The viceroys, including the famous Lord Mountbatten (who pondered the last details of Independence and Partition here in 1947), made it their summer capital.

The old reasons to head for the hills still make a trip to Simla more than valid, even if the old viceregal glamour has gone. The air here is sweet, cool, and clear, and the pleasure of the quaint and tranquil English village atmosphere remains, along with some lovely walks into the surrounding mountains. You should, however, acclimatize to the altitude before attempting any long hikes.

In town, visitors can retrace the favorite promenades along the **Mall** and see the old administrative offices of the **Ridge**. The place at which these two meet is what Kipling called "Scandal Point." At the eastern end of the Mall you can see the **Gaiety Theatre**, one-time home of the Simla Amateur Dramatic Company, which is famous for its productions of Victorian drama and Edwardian operetta.

The Ridge leads past the Neo-Gothic, Anglican **Christ Church**, where the bells are made from the brass of cannons captured from the Sikhs. At the end of the Ridge, you'll find the baronial pile of **Viceregal Lodge**, nowadays used by the Institute for Advanced Studies. You can imagine rickshaws pulling up onto the grounds of the ivy-covered grey stone mansion for one of the viceroy's banquets. Peer into the grand hall, which has an elegant fireplace, a coffered ceiling, and a majestic staircase. Then continue to the top of **Jakko Hill**, where you can see a fine view of the town and valley.

Kashmir

The Vale of Kashmir, 1,700 m (5,000 ft) above sea level, has historically offered much-needed respite for conquerors and travelers alike. Passing through the deserts of Sind and the hot and dusty plains of the Ganga valley, they have heard tell of its blessed meadows, forests, full fruit orchards, and lakes. It remains the undisputed treasure of the entire sub-continent. Unfortunately, continuing tensions between India and Pakistan in the region have rendered Kashmir a dangerous place for travellers.

In accordance with the U.S. State Department's and British Foreign Office's travel advisories, as well as warnings issued by most other foreign consulates, we do not recommend Kashmir as a tourist destination. The following information is provided only for the sake of background on the area.

Many people in the past, particularly during high summer, made Kashmir the principal destination of their visit to India,

The Himalayas, mountains of uncommon beauty, are one of the world's best skiing sites.

combining it with perhaps just brief outings and day-trips in Delhi and Agra. Those making more extensive tours of India, planned to see Kashmir at the end, with the intention of relaxing in a houseboat on a lake or going on a refreshing hike in the lush surrounding mountains.

Travel to Kashmir used to require bookings and preparations far in advance of visiting. But since the increase in eruptions of violence over the past ten years, foreign travel to the region has greatly decreased. During Kashmir's height of popularity as a tourist destination, one of the area's most alluring features was the unique accommodation on houseboats. Travel agencies can reserve a houseboat for a couple of days, allowing travellers to change around once they've fully settled in. One important and major advantage of advance reservations is that the visitor will be met at the airport straight away by a representative of the houseboat-owner—it's not easy for newcomers to find their way among the boats.

Houseboats are a beautifully preserved tradition of the heyday of the British Raj. In the 19th century, when Kashmir was the most exotic hill-station of them all, the maharaja forbade the British to buy land there, so they then hit on the brilliant alternative of building luxuriously appointed houseboats moored on the lakes near Srinagar. Equipped with all the Victorian upper-middle class comforts the colonials were used to, the more maneuverable, smaller houseboats made their way to other lakes for duck-shoots or just for the pleasures of the cruise, while the larger ones stayed languidly put.

With so many new boats having been built in the same old style, boasting lovely Kashmiri carvings on the bridge and decks, many are too heavy to move around the waters. But the traditional com-

The houseboats on Dal Lake, most built in the lovely old Kashmiri style, are surprisingly plush and exceedingly comfortable.

forts are the same: wood-burning stoves, plush armchairs in the living room, warm carpeting in the spacious bedrooms, superb personal service, and fine Kashmiri cuisine you can enjoy on deck—note that you can arrange with the owner what you want to eat each day, Western or Indian style.

Most houseboats are moored on Dal Lake, but for those seeking seclusion, there are others on the smaller Nagin Lake to the west. They are well serviced by *shikaras*—gaily decorated and roofed canoes somewhat reminiscent of Venetian gondolas—plying their way around the lake, ferrying passengers. There is also a floating market of fruit and flowers. The shikaras will also show you carpets, silks, shawls, brassware, jewels, and carvings—and tailors' establishments with names like Savile Roy, recalling their old British allegiance.

A study in contrasts: this sunny valley full of yellow colza is nestled at the base of the rugged Himalayas.

Srinagar

Srinagar, like Jammu and the rest of Kashmir, is still considered a dangerous place for foreign travellers. There is a strong military presence in the city and a dusk-till-dawn curfew is often in effect. The heart of Kashmir's capital is built along the banks of the serpentine Jhelum river on the southern shore of the lakes. The many bazaars, busy tailor's shops, and government-operated emporiums are fascinating places to observe the style, panache, and never-ending gall of that charming and often shameless scoundrel, the Kashmiri merchant.

Few monuments have survived Kashmir's troubled history, but the city's beauty lies in its numerous tranquil lakes and gardens. **Dal Lake** and the adjoining **Nagin** offer leisurely cruises, with passengers lounging on the cushions of a shikara. Lovely **floating gardens** growing melons, tomatoes, cucumbers, and lotus root in a

Beautiful Bone of Contention

Alexander left Greek settlements guarding the western frontiers of Kashmir, and thus Greeks filtered into the mountain kingdom. Emperor Ashoka is said to have sent Buddhist missionaries to found the town of Srinagar in the third century B.C.

In medieval times, Kashmir remained, with a brief Mongol interlude, under Hindu kings until Afghans conquered it in the name of Islam in the 14th century. With their equal enthusiasm for both iconoclasm and creativity, they smashed the Hindu temples and introduced the arts of silk weaving, shawl embroidery, wood carving, and ornamental papier mâché that have been the glory of Kashmir ever since.

Kashmir flourished under the Mughals, Akbar appreciating the sweet fruits of its orchards that he missed in the plains, and Jahangir and Shahjahan laying out gardens that provoked the envy of Louis XIV when he heard about them. The Persian plunderer, Nadir Shah, couldn't resist laying claim to Kashmir but was soon replaced again by the Afghans. Supreme indignity for the Muslims came with the Sikh conquest led by Ranjit Singh in 1819.

The British did not help matters much when, nearly 30 years later, they took the state away from the Sikhs and handed it to a Hindu Rajput prince, under British protection, with Muslims forming an overwhelming majority of the population (today 68%). Muslim invaders tried to overthrow the Hindu ruler in 1947 and the latter, Maharaja Hari Singh, was rescued by the Indian Army only on condition that he agreed to Kashmir's joining India rather than Pakistan.

With hostility between India and Pakistan unresolved since a brief war over Kashmir in 1965, no simple solution seems in sight. Today, with two-thirds of the original state in Indian hands and the other third, to the north and west, under Pakistani rule, many Kashmiris have a plague-on-both-your-houses attitude, remaining, in spirit if not in political fact, resolutely independent.

mesh of reeds and mud floating in the water and moored in squares by four poles stuck in the lake bed, add to the tranquil beauty of the lake.

On the western shore of Dal Lake, is the large white dome and minarets of **Hazratbal Mosque**, famous for its relic, the hair of the beard of the prophet Mohammed.

There are two small squares of land that rise up out of the lake: Sonalank, Akbar's Golden Island to the north, and Ruplank, Silver Island, to the south.

Two hills, **Hari Parbat** to the north of town and **Shankaracharya** to the east, offer pleasant walks—with the reward of a magnificent view over the lakes and the whole Vale of Kashmir, 134 km long and 40 km wide (82 by 25 miles).

The **Mughal Gardens** are on the eastern shore of Dal Lake. For Jahangir, if the Islamic idea of paradise had any meaning, it was here, amid the staggered terraces, tranquil pools, waterfalls, and trees, looking out over the lake against the backdrop of the Himalayas. In summer, there's a sound-and-light show at Jahangir's favorite, the **Shalimar Bagh**, laid out in the year 1616. Visitors are able to relax here as the emperor did, by lingering on the terraces to take in the changing scene that surround them. The white marble pavilion on the first terrace was used for public audiences, the second was a private pavilion, the third—made from black marble—accommodated the harem, and the fourth was strictly reserved for the emperor's private use.

Three km (2 miles) to the south, **Nishat Bagh** was laid out in 1633 by Asaf Khan, the brother of Jahangir's wife. It is the largest of the gardens, with 12 terraces and lined with fine cedars and cypresses. It offers a magnificent view of the lake beyond.

Tucked away in a small fold of the hills is **Chashma Shahi**, the smallest but in many ways most exquisite of the Mughal Gardens, drawing its water from a spring that runs directly down the adjacent mountainside.

Harvesting the floating gardens on Dal Lake: here, water-bound farmers bring in the lotus leaves.

Excursions from Srinagar

The resort **Pahalgam** is about 95 km (60 miles) east of Srinagar. The route there runs through groves of willow, used for the local cricket-bat industry, and fields of saffron. If you've ever wondered why saffron is so expensive, it's because 150,000 of these purple or white crocuses (only the stamen is orange) are necessary to make up a single kilogram (2 pounds) of saffron proper, the stuff that flavors and colors those famous Indian curries and Spanish *paella*. (Spain is the only other place in the world apart from Kashmir where saffron is grown extensively.)

The most popular journey from Pahalgam is 45 km (27 miles) up to the **Amarnath Cave**, which has an altitude of some 3,895 m (12,742 ft). Sacred to Hindus, it is a destination of devout pilgrimage on festive days for the sight of the imposing stalagmite called Shiva's *lingam*; this phallic symbol stands for the god's fertility, power, and creativity. Just 35 km (22 miles) from Pahalgam, one trek, the most strenuous by far, leads to the spectacular **Kolahoi Glacier**.

Gulmarg, 52 km (32 miles) west of Srinagar, is about 2,653 m (8,622 ft) above sea level. It is currently developing its winter sports in addition to the golf and tennis already provided. There is wonderful hiking here, too, through pine forests and meadows carpeted with wildflowers in summer.

THE WEST

The West is, above all, Rajasthan, land of the great maharajas, with its desert and lake palaces, but it's also the bustle of Mumbai and the

splendor of the cave temples at Ajanta and Ellora. There is also the great bonus, further down the coast, of the stunning beaches of Goa.

Introducing Rajasthan

Rajasthan is undoubtedly one of the most romantic regions in India. Known as Rajputana, and stretching from Delhi to the Pakistani Sind and the Punjab, this land is where the Rajput warriors erected their desert and mountain redoubts. The palace-fortresses were built with granite from the surrounding hills, and with the same dazzling marble used for the Taj Mahal.

The great cities of Jaisalmer and Jodhpur are on the ancient caravan routes from the Indus Valley to the Thar Desert, for this is a land of cattle-herders too. One of their most spectacular monuments is the annual market-festival at Pushkar held each year in November (see page 209).

Probably descendants of the invading Scythians and Huns, the Rajputs were a formidable opposition met by the waves of invaders —Turks, Afghans, and Mughals. Despite the Rajputs' "foreign" origin, their claimed "descendancy" from the Aryan dynasties of the sun and moon was accepted by the Brahman priesthood and they were duly inducted retroactively into the Kshatriya warrior caste, a caste to which the Rajputs of today continue proudly to belong.

While the nearby Malwa and Gujarat came under Muslim rule, Rajputana remained Hindu. Towns with the suffix *-pur* had Hindu rulers; *-abad* is the Muslim suffix. Some Rajput princes pursued an independent line. Others sent their daughters to the harem or their sons to serve as officers in the imperial army. They enjoyed a privileged position during the time of the British Raj.

Elephants line up like taxis would in some big metropolis to carry visitors around Amber fort.

Ladies discreetly watched the goings-on below, invisible behind the Hawa Majal windows.

Jaipur

The capital of Rajasthan was built according to astrological precepts. Raja Jai Singh II, that scholar of the stars who dotted northern India with his collections of instruments for observing the heavens, chose an exact date for moving his capital from Amber—17 November 1727—as auspicious. He then laid it out according to the disposition of the stars and planets.

But let's begin at **Amber**, 9 km (5 miles) northeast of Jaipur, high up on a hill commanding a gorge, which offered military advantage but was not right for the expanded city he wanted for his capital.

The road up to Amber takes you through classical Rajasthani landscape, its parched hills embracing Lake Maota, where water buffalo snooze lazily in the sun. You may also pass an occasional camel, that time-honored vehicle of transport known as the "ship of the desert," hauling his load on a cart fitted with discarded tires from an airplane.

At the **fortress**, the Rajputs of Jai Singh's Kachwaha clan slowed down their enemies with a steep elephant ramp. You can travel by elephant up through the Suraj Pol (Sun Gate) to the **Jaleb Chauk**, a garden courtyard swarming with langur monkeys and surrounded by elephant stables.

A staircase zigzags its way to the **Temple of Kali** (wife of Shiva), built for the Hindu mother-goddess. The silver doors have bas-relief panels depicting Kali riding various animals. Her statue was brought from Bengal, where the cult of Kali is particularly strong. The **palace** is a subtle example of the maharajas' opulence: artists banished by Emperor Aurangzeb (see page 41) worked on the columns and arches, and on the building's gallery around the **Diwan-i-Am** (Hall of Public Audience).

The Diwan-i-Khas (the Private Audience Chamber), known as the **Shish Mahal** (Palace of Mirrors), features the Rajputs' flamboyant taste for covering walls with green, orange, and purple glass, and the vaulted ceilings with thousands of little convex mirrors. Strike a match to see the effect.

This musician's ancestor may have once entertained the Rajputs in Jaipur's Amber.

The most inviting place in the palace is the **Sukh Niwas** (Hall of pleasure), with doors inlaid in ivory and sandalwood. Inside, cool water was brought down from the roof through a carved white marble chute, and fresh air was brought in through the finely chiselled lattice stonework. The color of its sandstone has earned for Jaipur the name "pink city"—although you will see that it changes color with the season and time of day, from a rosy pink to warmest amber, bright orange, and dull ochre.

Appropriate for a descendant of the sun dynasty, Jai Singh laid out the city on an axis from the **Suraj Pol** (Sun Gate) in the east to the **Chand Pol** (Moon Gate) in the west, a main street that is today a lively bazaar.

The town's central focus was the most elaborate **Jantar Mantar** observatory, which was the final fruit of his labors and begun in Delhi (see page 74). The initiated will appreciate the significance, others the mysterious atmosphere of its cream-colored gnomons (the uprights of sundials), quadrants, and sextants.

Chandra Mahal, directly south of the observatory, is the City's Palace, with seven mys-

Elephants being the primary form of transportation, fortresses were fitted with elephant ramps; you can still travel through Amber this way.

tically planned courtyards and stories. A museum inside the building gives intriguing insight into the life and heyday of the maharajas: their rich costumes, their scimitars, and rifles inlaid with bright jewels and silver—and a horrible bludgeon with a double serrated edge.

Overlooking the street is the **Hawa Mahal**, literally the Wind Palace, but actually a rather grand, five-storied royal box, in which the ladies could sit and watch festive processions. Its airy, projecting oriel-shaped balconies are seen as a symbolic image of Jaipur style. There's a fine view from the top of the zigzag staircase.

Jodhpur

Of all Rajasthan's fortifications, Jodhpur's **Fort**, perched high on its sheer cliffs at the eastern edge of the Thar Desert, must surely rank among the most imposing. The Rathor Rajputs, always a belligerent bunch and bad trouble for Mughal foes and the Rajputs, built it in the 15th century. Akbar decided it was better to have them on his side than to try to convert them; when he married the Maharaja of Jodhpur's sister, Jodh Bai (for whom he built a grand palace at Fatehpur Sikri; see page 84) there was no question of converting her to Islam.

Near the east gate, you'll see tombstones where soldiers died defending the fort, and cannonball scars indicating efforts by Maharaja of Jaipur to snatch a promised bride, Princess Krishna Kumari, against her will; she took her own life during the battle. On top of the ramparts the fort displays its proudest possessions: a set of fierce-looking howitzers and a few cannons. From here there is a fine view of the blue-and-whitewashed city.

Behind the ramparts and the gates with sharp iron spikes to stop elephants from ramming them, there is a very handsome residential

Land Survey at the Gallop

Jai Singh traced his ancestry back to the sun dynasty of Ayodhya with a grand sense of tradition. He asserted his independence from the Mughal empire by reviving the ancient Indo-Aryan practice of the asvamedha, or royal horse sacrifice. By this ritual, a king used to lay claim to all the land covered by a sacred white stallion let loose to roam for one year, followed by his army.

Any neighboring king who objected to his land being claimed in this way had to fight for the right to his own land. As a reward for its efforts, the stallion was mated, symbolically, with the king's wives and then cut up into quarters for a sacrificial meal.

The Rajputs outdid the Mughals with their taste in riotous color, imbedding walls with bright glass and even bits of mirror.

palace. Its majesty is most notable in the balconies of the **Royal Harem**, which have screens of the most delicate latticework. The palace **museum** displays a colorful collection of exhibits, giving insight into the daily life of those who lived there. There are luxuriously embroidered elephant howdahs as well as babies' cradles and ladies' palanquins. A version of a sedan-chair, palanquins were either completely closed up so that a promised bride was invisible while inside, or constructed with a peep hole to allow her to see out — and be seen for — when she was married.

At the **Iron Gate** exit, you'll see a more poignant side of the life of a maharaja's wife — 15 scarlet sati handprints on the wall, from widows who threw themselves onto their husbands' funeral pyres in ritual sacrifice, in keeping with the tradition of the era.

In the bustling old center of Jodhpur itself, you can't and shouldn't miss the **Saddar Market** situated by the old clock-tower. Any one of a dozen barbers will be happy to give you a shave and a haircut under the banyan tree—and you'll get a good deal of local gossip in the bargain. In the market proper, spices and grain are piled up in multi-colored mountains; merchants chant as they measure out separate lots of five kilos each: "three, three, three," "four, four, four," and "five, five, five." And the fort always looms on the horizon, a constant reminder of the town's war-torn history.

Just 8 km (5 miles) due north of Jodhpur, the maharajas' mausoleum is in a pretty park on the site of the old capital of **Mandor**. Watched over by crows, pigeons, and parakeets—and some rare birds, which will doubtlessly be of interest only to ornithologists—are a number of temple-like memorials built on the site of the maharajas' funeral pyres, and a colonnade of Hindu god-heroes.

If you're going to Jaisalmer by road, it's well worth a detour to **Osian** to see the stunning Hindu and Jain temples, many of them dating as far back as the eighth century. Somehow this ancient sculpted pantheon of Hindu deities and Jain prophets has survived

What, No Jodhpurs?

Those celebrated tapered riding breeches were in fact the fashion of hunters all over northern India, but it was the Maharaja of Jodhpur who brought them to London, for Queen Victoria's Diamond Jubilee celebrations. Or rather, he didn't bring them—they got lost in a shipwreck and he had to get a London tailor to make him a new pair. The secret of their peculiar design was out and they became all the rage among English horsemen, along with the dapper maharaja's ankle-length riding boots, also known as jodhpurs, and his close-fitting Jodhpuri coat.

The dream-like landscape of the sandstone fort of Jaisalmer recalls the Arabia of biblical times.

the sometimes ferocious weather of India and Mahmud of Ghazni's iconoclasts.

Back on the road to Jaisalmer, one last splash of color delights the senses before you plunge into the desert: the fields are dotted with mounds of red hot chili peppers.

Jaisalmer

Situated on the route of the ancient caravans that brought goods from the Middle East and Central Asia, the sandstone citadel of Jaisalmer, protected by an imposing double set of bastions, rises like a mirage from the sands of the Thar Desert.

Jaisalmer, founded by the Maharawals in 1156, is the oldest of Rajasthan's fortified cities. Though much of the city has grown up outside the **fort**—modern in time, but not in style—3,000 people

The intricately carved sandstone exteriors of Jaisalmer's balconies are just one element in the magic of the place.

live within its walls. Some of their houses in the side streets are from the 12th century. The best view of the whole citadel can be had from the terrace of the Jaisal Castle Hotel.

The elaborate sculpture in four 15th-century **Jain temples** within the fort finds its counterpart in the finely carved façades of the **Merchants' Havelis** (mansions), built 200 years later, and sheltered from sandstorms on the northeast side. But much more than the individual monuments—handsome but hardly grandiose, because of the restricted spaces available—it is the general atmosphere of the town that gives it its special magic. Everything here is bathed in a serene desert light that adds a shimmer to the stone and a translucence to the shadows. To see the **desert** at its best, go out at dawn and at sunset.

Beyond Jaisalmer, you'll find the road peters out at the village of Sam and the forbidden area of Indian military installations on the border with Pakistan. On the way to the village you'll come across a "camel-station," from where you may wish to take a ride. For fans of this quaint form of transport, longer camel safaris can be set up through Jaisalmer travel agencies. Ask the camel driver to direct you to the still uncharted village of **Kuldhara**—uncharted because it was one of 84 villages abandoned over 160 years ago by the clan of Paliwal Brahmins, who, after living there for centuries, left suddenly during the night, rather than having to face paying the new, arbitrary land-tax. It still stands as a ghost town—groups of dilapidated square houses made from sandstone—and is visited nowadays only by the occasional goatherd, who will play you a tune on his flute in traditional style.

Just 9 km (5 miles) out of town, **Mool Sagar** gardens are a popular place for picnics in the rainy season. There are pretty arbors and a monsoon pavilion, but it is in fact pleasant all year round.

Titles and Titles

Rajput princes attached great importance to titles. At first they were known as Rao or Rana ("chief" or "chieftain") of their clan. Akbar made them happy by calling them Raja ("King"). From there, they promoted themselves to Maharaja ("Great King") or, higher ranking, Maharana, then Maharaja Dhiraj ("Great King of Kings"), and even Maharaja Dhiraj Raj Rajesur (something like "Great Hero King of all Kings"). You might have thought it would stop there. But no, then came the British, with their "Knight of the Garter," "Knight Commander of the British Empire," and the rest.

The princes began to count how many titles they could collect, the all-important thing being the number of initials each contained. A state crisis might arise if somebody got only a CVO (Companion of the Victorian Order) when his rival was a KCVO (Knight Companion etc.). The Maharaja of Jaipur, for instance, died happy in 1970 as Lieutenant-General HH Maharaja Sir Man Singh Bahadur, GCSI, GCIE.

Udaipur

If Jaisalmer is the city of the desert, then Udaipuri is is its opposite: the city of lakes and gardens. The lakes were created by the Maharana Udai Singh for his new capital by damming up the Berach river after Akbar had ransacked his mountain redoubt at Chittorgarh.

The Maharanas of Udaipur had five palaces in and around Udaipur: the City Palace for winter quarters; the Jagniwas in Lake Pichola used as a summer palace (now the Lake Palace Hotel); the Jag Mandir on Pichola, used for festivals; the Lakshmi Vilas Palace for guests beside lake Fateh Sagar; and a monsoon palace up in the Aravalli Hills. It was the marble used for them that Shahjahan chose for his Taj Mahal.

Lake Pichola, 4 km (2 miles) long and 3 km (2 miles) wide is the largest. Cruises are available from the Bhansi Ghat, which is near

The stunning city of Udaipur boasts five palaces, all built from the fine marble later chosen for construction of the Taj Mahal.

This water-carrier is forever wading through Pichola, one of Udaipur's many lakes.

the City Palace. This will enable you to travel out to the **Lake Palace Hotel**, even if you're not staying there. The southern end of Pichola has the best **view** of the lake, taking in the two island-palaces and the City Palace beyond.

The 16th-century **City Palace** on the east shore of the lake is now part royal residence, part luxury hotel, and part museum. The sun symbol of the maharana is everywhere, worshiped during monsoons. The armor displayed here includes an outfit for disguising horses as elephants. The frescoes illustrate the tragic story of Princess Krishna's suicide at Jodhpur. Glass baubles, some as big as golf balls, have replaced real jewels in the mosaics.

North of the City Palace is the handsome **Jagdish Temple**, a rare example of Indo-Aryan style and symbol of its independent spirit. The **Bharatiya Lokkala Mandal Folk Museum** has an excellent display of Rajasthani art, which includes bright puppets, costumes, and the whole range of turbans worn by the various Rajput clans. A modest puppet show is put on every 20 to 25 minutes in the puppet theater.

Fateh Sagar Lake is reached by boat at the north end of Pichola, but you can also get there by a pleasant drive past the gardens of bougainvillaea and lilac of Lakshmi Vilas Palace.

You can visit the **Gardens of Saheliyon-ki-Bari** (Maids of Honor), where the maharana kept the Muslim dancers presented to him by the Mughal emperor. The gardens here are famous for their five fountains that imitate the many different sounds of the monsoon, from light showers to torrential storms.

Chittorgarh, a fortress, was the site of the Rajputs' many acts of sacrifice. Making the trip by road or rail from Udaipur, it is on a plateau some 150 m (487 ft) in height up in the Aravalli Hills.

Entering the northwestern side, you can go through seven gateways to see the remains of the Rajput's heroic exploits. Stones mark where each of these brave soldiers fell in battle.

South of the Main Gate, the 15th-century **Palace of Kumbha**, is built over the cave where Padmini led the first *jauhar* and to which the Rajputs' descendants return for an annual celebration. Some of the walls in the palace were built with pieces of stone removed from Buddhist temples.

Kumbha's **Jaya Stambha** (the Tower of Victory), 37 m (120 ft)

high, was built to celebrate his great victory over Sultan Mahmud Khalji of Malwa in 1440. The tower's nine stories are decorated with Hindu deities, but otherwise it seems inspired by the **Kirti Stambha**, a Jain Tower of Fame, built in the 12th century.

At the southern end, beside a pond with a pavilion in the middle, is **Padmini's Palace**, where the princess is said to have passed her last days. It is unlikely that the mirror in the room overlooking the pond was the very one in which the sultan got

The camel is the faithful guardian of Rajasthan's deepest mystery: the desert.

his fatal peek at her, but the guides tell the story this way to make it more enticing for visitors.

☛ Ranakpur

Hills and mountains are especially sanctified in the cult of Jainism. In fact, in the Aravalli Hills, situated in the southwestern part of Rajasthan, you will find one of the Jains' leading sanctuaries. North of Udaipur, a mountain road takes you past green terraced fields and mango groves over the deepest ravines to the magnificent white marble temple complex of Ranakpur.

Chaumukha Temple is known nowadays as the quadruple temple because of its four central domes within a complex of 84 domed shrines, each one topped by a flag with tinkling bells attached— paying musical homage to the many deities worshiped inside. Built in 1438, the Chaumukha is dedicated to Adinath, Jainism's original 24 Tirthankaras (teachers), whose truths were revealed by the prophet Mahavira (see page 85).

Do or Die

Rajput warriors placed a horrifyingly high price on their honor. In 1303, Sultan Ala-ud-Din of Delhi laid siege to Chittorgarh, it is said, to win for himself the Princess Padmini, whose beauty he had been allowed only a glimpse of in a mirror. Rather than submit, the Rajputs' wives and daughters committed jauhar, mass self-immolation, while the warriors rode out of the fort in the saffron robes traditionally worn for the last battle unto death.

Over 200 years later came another heroic resistance against the Sultan of Gujarat, ending in another tragic jauhar, in which 13,000 women are said to have died along with 32,000 saffron-clad Rajputs. The last stand came with the devastating attack by Akbar in 1567, and one final suicidal sacrifice and battle.

As with all the holy places of Jainism, you must remove not only your shoes but any leather you may be wearing. Walking through the entrance hall—which is decorated with a number of sensual sculptures—and across the half-moon threshold, you penetrate a forest of symmetrical pillars, each subtly different in its intricate carving. The 15th-century temple's rich carvings attest to the wealth of the Jain merchant who commissioned it. You can find a sculpture of him in a position of prayer facing the statue of Adinath, in the second row of pillars, second pillar from the left. His architect, Deepa, is also here, in the third row of pillars, first pillar on the right. Restoration work on the temple is, amazingly, carried out by the 14th generation of Deepa's direct descendants. You can climb up to the roof for a fascinating perspective of the flags, domes, and trees surrounded by the Aravalli Hills.

The Dilwara Temples are located on **Mount Abu**, in a former hill-station for the British (now used by the Indian bourgeoisie). If you go—and the temples are well worth it—you would do best to take the train from Jaipur or Ahmedabad.

Ajanta and Ellora

The cave temples hewn from the granite of the Vindhya mountains in the northwest of Deccan are among the great wonders of India. They are considered masterpieces, because the "caves" are actually man-made hollows in solid rock, from which a complex of architecturally elaborate temples and monasteries has been carved with simple instruments. Even beyond this tour de force, the rock-cut sanctuaries of Ajanta and Ellora are superb works of art, boasting sensuous painting and expressive sculpture of the highest order.

Both temples are within easy reach of the town of Aurangabad. Try not to visit both sites on the same day. If you are interested in following the historical evolution of the temples, stop off at Ajanta first, where some caves are from the second century B.C. Reserve Ellora for a tour during the afternoon, when the caves will

Ajanta cave-painting depicts the sensual life that Buddha chose to leave behind him.

be illuminated by sunlight. Reliable official guides from the office of the Archaeological Survey of India offer their services free of charge.

Having remained untouched for 1,000 years, until British soldiers discovered it during a tiger hunt in 1819, **Ajanta** has the advantage over Ellora, whose caves were in constant use as dwelling places. The use of rock-cut sanctuaries goes back to the time of Emperor Ashoka, during the third century B.C., when itinerant Buddhist monks formed a religious order and the emperor provided them with rock-hewn cells as a *vihara* (retreat) during the monsoons. The monks added a hall for worship called a *chaitya* (temple).

Of the 29 caves, all of them Buddhist, five are chaitya temples and the rest vihara monasteries. They are cut from a horseshoe-shaped cliff standing 75 m (252 ft) high above a narrow gorge, which has a small stream running through it. Originally, each vihara had its own stairway down to the stream. The caves have been numbered from 1 to 29, west to east. Experiencing just nine of them will give an impression of the whole. Start in the middle, at the oldest, then work your way east before returning to the historically later caves at the western entrance.

Cave 10 is probably the oldest of the chaitya temples, dated at about 150 B.C. Its nave and aisles are divided by 39 octagonal pillars leading to a *stupa*, the domed focus of veneration, with an apse beyond, permitting the circumambulation. There is no representation of the Buddha in this early era.

Cave 9, a sanctuary from the first century B.C., is smaller than number 10. It is dominated by the stupa. The two-story façade with arched window and Buddha figures in side niches was probably added in the sixth century A.D.

Two elephants in a kneeling position welcome you to **Cave 16**, one of the most important of the later caves, created between A.D. 475 and A.D. 600. The Mahayana school of Buddhism encouraged worship of a Buddha image, which is why the stupa was replaced with a sculpture of Buddha sitting in a posture used traditionally for teaching. Look for the two sculptures of amorous couples on the ceiling.

With the richness and vigor of its mural paintings, **Cave 17** represents the summit of Ajanta's artistry. The walls, from the fifth century A.D., show the 12 stories of Buddha's enlightenment. Buddha's steadfast resistance to temptation gave the painters of that time a splendid pretext to show the sensual side of court life as a foil to the Master's spirituality. We see him taming an enraged elephant or appearing as the warrior Simhala attacking the Island of Ogresses, while his wife Rani, holding a mirror, languorously prepares her toilet with handmaidens holding her cosmetics.

The sculpted Buddha is seen with the wheel, symbolic of his law, and two deer, referring to the park at Sarnath where he held his first sermon. Look for two smaller figures on the pedestal, one of which is holding a bowl for alms or offerings—they represent the rich merchants who financed the cave's construction.

The small chaitya of **Cave 19** is notable for the carved façade and Buddha statues in its interior and for the graceful figures relaxing in the side niches at the entrance. Visit **Cave 26** for a riot of "architectural" bravura—the elaborately ribbed vaulting, finely carved pillars, and a truly Baroque shrine with seated Buddha.

Unlike the early, rather austere monasteries, **Caves 1 and 2** are richly ornamented. There are superb murals of bright-eyed deer, peacocks, monkeys, and elephants, and also those depicting the opulent life, with Prince Siddhartha riding away on horseback. The masterpieces, though, are in Cave 1: two spiritual Bodhisattvas on the back wall on either side of the antechamber.

The caves of **Ellora** are cut out of a whole hillside of basalt rock, and conceived on a much grander scale than Ajanta's. Local villagers have relied on them as shelter during monsoons or epidemics, so the murals have disappeared, but the magnificent sculpture has survived. Starting where Ajanta left off—some of the

Buddhist artists may well have moved over to Ellora— all of the 34 caves were created between the seventh and 12th centuries. The first 12 are Buddhist, 17 are Hindu, and the other five are Jain. They stretch north–south over 3 km (2 miles), allowing you the option of climbing behind some of them as well as approaching from the cave entrance.

The most important Buddhist excavation (1–12) is the only chaitya sanctuary here, the eighth-century **Cave 10** with its

This temple was not built from the ground up, but hewn from a granite cliff.

fine rib-vaulted ceiling reminiscent of a western Romanesque cathedral. The great Buddha seated in the domed stupa is worshiped by Hindu artisans as Visvakarma, carpenter of the gods, so the sanctuary is known as the "Cave of the Carpenters."

Cave 12 consists of a vihara dormitory with three stories. Its sensual, feminine sculptures show significant Tantric Hindu influence. You must imagine these as they were originally painted, in brilliant colors.

Of the Hindu temples (13–29), **Cave 14** is an interesting transition from the Buddhist caves, because in the pantheon of Hindu gods, Vishnu sits in a meditative pose, suggesting he was converted from a Buddha. Another two are similar to the Bodhisattvas of Ajanta. The sculpture shows a dynamic Shiva killing demons and playing

dice in the Himalayas, a group of boys playing with the sacred bull, and mother goddesses with children.

 The masterpiece of Ellora is the **Kailasa Temple** of **Cave 16**. With a ground plan the size of the Greek Parthenon and a structure half as tall again, this was the work of the eighth-century Deccan king Krishna I. In the process of shaping the temple and its shrines in an area 82 m (265 ft) long and some 47 m (150 ft) wide, leaving the back "wall" of the courtyard 30 m (97 ft) high, an amazing 200,000 tons of rock were cut away from the face of the hill. Whatever was saved in hauling the masonry needed to "erect" such an edifice was more than counter-balanced by the seven generations of craftsmen who completed their amazing carvings from one piece of rock. The anonymous sculptors created a panoply of Hindu tradition —legendary heroes and their battles, hunts, and weddings.

The result is a Hindu temple on a grand scale which can be easily compared with its inspiration: the many temples of Mahabalipuram (see page 194), built some 50 years before in the southern region. The huge gateway leads to the *mandapa* worship hall, with the tall pyramid of the shrine beyond, the whole structure symbolizing the mythical Mount Meru, Himalayan home of the gods.

Cut and Paste

As you can see from unfinished caves such as 14 or 24, the sanctuaries were "created downwards," scooped out of the cliff from top to bottom rather than being built up from floor to roof. Deviation from conventional architecture makes it more appropriate to speak of monumental sculpture: roof-beams, columns, and arches did not have to serve their usual weight-bearing functions.

The wall paintings are sometimes wrongly described as frescoes, in which paint is applied to a damp plastered surface. The technique used in this case, however, is that of tempera, paint applied to a dried surface of plastered cow-dung.

After seeing the sculpted friezes at courtyard level, you can gain yet another perspective of the temple's fine detail from above, by walking along the stone ledge that leads around the top. Do wear good shoes and use the safety railing.

After Kailasa, the Jain caves (numbers 30–34), excavated between the eighth and 13th centuries, will come as an anti-climax — and this despite the considerable prowess of their sculptors.

Cave 31 tries to emulate the style of the great Hindu temple on a much smaller scale, but the artists here were working on much harder rock and so abandoned their effort. The most interesting of all remains the two-story **Cave 32**, known as Indra Sabha, notable for the upper floor's extravagant carving — the hallmark of Jain sculptors — and the great stone elephant, more rigid than Kailasa's (because of the tougher stone), but somehow more noble.

Mumbai (Bombay)

"Gateway of India" still describes the main function of Mumbai, known until 1995 as Bombay. For those who want to work their way down to the south, Mumbai is still, as it was for the servants and soldiers of the British Empire, the natural gateway.

An occasional luxury liner still glides past the great stone gateway, the harbor promenade of the Apollo Bunder, and the Yacht Club to dock at Ballard Pier. For the rest of us landing at Santacruz Airport, the old turmoil of dockside porters and rickshaws that once submerged the newcomer has been replaced by the equally crazy bustle of businessmen and workers going to and from the Gulf. With skyscrapers shooting up almost every month, Mumbai is the busiest industrial and commercial center in India — cars, textiles, chemicals, nuclear energy, and shipping — and a focus for the cinema and the renewal of Indian art. But this huge wealth is juxtaposed with abject poverty, epitomized by women carrying bricks on their heads to build luxury apartments, and sackcloth hovels on construction sites.

For anyone who is not here on business, three days, at most four, should be enough to get a good idea of this exhausting city—with the possible exception of nostalgics of the British Raj, who will find a wealth of intriguing relics.

Before exploring the sprawl that stretches in a wide crescent over 20 km (12 miles) from north to south, go to the Government of India Tourist Information Office, situated opposite Churchgate Station. Then begin just where King George V himself did on his visit back in 1911, on the promontory at the end of Apollo Bunder. This site is marked today by the world famous **Gateway of India**—a monument moving for its symbolism more than its beauty (depending on how you feel about the British Empire it was built to celebrate).

Kipling insisted in his *Ballad of East and West* that "never the twain shall meet," but the British have done their best, perching four Gujarati domes on this otherwise very Roman concept of a triumphal arch. This edifice was inaugurated in the year 1924; the Somerset Light Infantry solemnly marched through it to their ships some 24 years later. They were the last British troops to leave India.

The Indian equestrian **statue of Shivaji** faces the gateway. It was erected in 1961 to honor the Maratha hero of Hindu nationalism who fought against the Mughals (see page 38). Beside him is the **Taj Mahal Hotel**, another monument built by a member of the Tatas, the Parsi industrialist dynasty. Architecturally, it is also a mixture of Western and oriental styles, and a surviving part of the traditional tour that took world travelers from the West to Shepheard's in Cairo, Raffles in Singapore, the Peninsula in Hong Kong, and the Imperial in Tokyo. You can get a whiff of the old romance by taking tea in the Sea Lounge and enjoying the harbor view—recall the dizzy *ingénue* in the bar who thought that the mausoleum at Agra was named after the hotel.

Mumbai's Dhobi Ghat is a sacred place, but also quite possibly the world's largest open-air laundry.

The "Gateway of India" is located in Mumbai—both literally and figuratively.

The Raj District

Northwest from the Taj, in the area around the Maidan that was the heart of British Bombay, connoisseurs appreciate the architecture that fans call "eclectic" and foes "mongrel."

The old Secretariat is mostly described as Venetian Gothic, the University Library French Gothic, the Telegraph Office Romanesque, and the High Court and the Cathedral of St. Thomas as Early English. The architects were British but the artisans were Indian—and adept at adding detail reminiscent of Rajput forts and Mughal palaces.

The national mood is stressed on the octagonal spire of the University's **Rajabai Clocktower**, with 24 figures representing the castes of the Maharashtra State, of which Mumbai is the capital. Even the most anti-imperialist may be touched in the **Cathedral**, by some of the poignant epitaphs for those who died in the military or civil service for their country. For big Raj-buffs, the supreme example of Indo-Gothic style is the *Victoria Terminus*, affectionately abbreviated to VT nowadays, once *the* railway station that launched adventures inland, now handling mostly suburban traffic.

Northwest of the VT is the bustling **Crawford Market** (known in post-Independence as Mahatma Jyotiba Phule). Behind the brick façade with bas-relief friezes by Kipling's father over the gate, the stalls retain their original layout: vegetables to the left; fruit and flowers to the right; and fish, mutton, and poultry straight ahead.

Kipling's Cradle

Rather than Delhi, Mumbai is the place for Raj buffs to start out, for this was the beginning of the British imperial adventure in India. Once just a chain of swampy, malaria-ridden islands inhabited by a few fishermen and peasants tapping toddy from the palm trees, it didn't seem a great loss to the Sultan of Gujarat when he ceded it to the Portuguese in 1534. They passed it on to the British as part of Catherine of Braganza's dowry to Charles II in 1661. The East India Company picked it up for a song at a rent of £10 a year for the next 62 years.

After years of intimidation by the Portuguese, the Hindu, Parsi, and Jewish merchants now flocked into the burgeoning port. The island-swamps were dried out and linked together by landfills to form one Bombay Island, separated from the mainland by the easily bridged Thana Creek. Modern docks were constructed, and the first cotton mills were completed in 1853, followed quickly by other factories to install Bombay's own industrial revolution. The bard of the Raj, Rudyard Kipling, son of the local art school teacher, was born here in 1865. Militarily, Bombay was British India's naval centre and, as you will see from the many warships in the harbor, remains today the headquarters of the Indian Navy.

The Indians' Mumbai

Beyond Crawford Market, the area that the Indians truly call their own—away from the Apollo Bunder and the Maidan and still redolent of their old imperial masters—is known in tribute to simple reality as the City. This is the heart of Mumbai's teeming street life, where Indians from the entire subcontinent compete with lively Maharashtrans in the **bazaars**. Among the extravagantly colored Hindu temples and subtle mosques in the Muslim neighborhoods, Jain merchants sell gold in the Zaveri Bazaar, while others sell silver, brass, copper, leather, and lace.

The Indians' Mumbai is also epitomized by the promenade of **Marine Drive**, around Back Bay from Nariman Point to the residential area of Malabar Hill.

One must-see is **Chowpatty Beach**, not for swimming or sunbathing, but because it is one of the greatest people-watching spots in western India: fakirs and fakers walk on fire, sleep on nails, climb ropes in midair, or bury their heads in the sand; food vendors hawk *kulfi* ice cream as well as *pan*, betel-chew, and *bhelpuri*, a spicy local specialty.

Museums

The **Prince of Wales Museum**, at the southern end of Mahatma Gandhi Road, has a collection of miniatures and seventh-century

---

Francis Xavier's Relics

Every ten years (the next time in 2004) the body of St. Francis Xavier is carried from the church of Bom Jesus to be exhibited at the cathedral. But not a lot is left. In 1554 a Portuguese lady bit a toe off; another toe fell off and is kept in a separate crystal box; the right hand was donated to the Catholic community in Nagasaki; and other pieces were sent to Rome.

Mumbai's museums hold both relics from the area's distant past and works of modern artists from the present.

sculptures from the caves of Elephanta, as well as a pottery and stone tools.

The new **Jehangir Art Gallery**, immediately behind the Museum, illustrates trends in modern Indian painting, including works by two of the most important artists from Mumbai, Tyeb Mehta and Akbar Padamsee.

In Victoria Gardens, don't miss the stone elephant from Elephanta Island; it belongs to the **Victoria and Albert Museum** nearby, a reminder of the old history of Imperial Bombay. More up-to-date, the Tourist Information Office can organize a visit to the set of a Mumbai **film studio** if you would like to watch one of their huge, romantic productions in progress.

Elephanta

The seventh-century cave-temples of Elephanta Island make a pleasant boat excursion by ferry from the Apollo Bunder; look for the nuclear reactors at Trombay. Known as Gharapuri, Sacred City of the Kings, the island was named Elephanta by Portuguese sailors. Although their musket practice damaged many sculptures of Hindu gods in the caves, enough survived to make it a worthwhile stop. Carved out of the rock mountain on the island, the caves may not seem impressive after visiting Ajanta and Ellora (see page 115), but the **Great Cave** is 40 m (130 ft) deep and 40 m wide. To the west stands Shiva's emblem.

On the rear wall is the **Shiva Mahesamurti**, a bust of Shiva as the Supreme Lord, while Bhairava the angry destroyer looks to the left and his sensuous aspect looks to the right. In a panel to the left is **Ardhanarishvara**, Shiva as both man and woman.

Goa

Time to relax—and this former Portuguese colony is the perfect place for it. The beaches are superb, offering all the white sands and palm trees you could wish for. The cuisine makes use of the best seafood in India, and the Goans, of mixed Hindu and Portuguese descent, are a lively community. There are also a few glazed-eyed latter-day hippies hanging on in the area, like relics of a bygone age.

Instead of flying down, many people prefer to take the more leisurely steamer from Mumbai. Embarkation takes place at the Alexandra Dock; the steamer boasts deluxe sleeping berths for your comfort during the 22-hour trip to the Goan capital city of Panaji (formerly Panjim). You will get a great look at the often dramatic mountains of the Western Ghats running parallel to the coast during your trip.

A view of the enchanting Arabian sea off the coast of Goa, colony of white-sand beaches and delicious seafood meals.

After Vasco da Gama landed on the Malabar Coast in 1498, the Portuguese invaded the area and seized Goa from the Sultan of Bijapur in the year 1510. They held the colony for the next 450 years, until finally Nehru launched an attack and drove them out.

Goa was a vital link for Portugal's colonial trade in the Indian Ocean. It also became a prime base for missionary activity, with its succession of devout followers of different faiths—the Franciscans, Augustinians, Dominicans, and the Jesuits—which held them in line along with a rigorous Inquisition most notably led by Francis Xavier, who came to Goa in the year 1542. The traders have now gone, but the missionaries' ancient churches in Velha Goa still stand, and make a fascinating sightseeing trip—that is if you can ever manage to tear yourself away from the paradisiacal beaches, which are so inviting.

The most popular beaches of all are **Calangute** and **Dona Paula**, each of them within reach of the capital, Panaji, and easy excursions out to Velha Goa. If you want to get away from the crowd, the most secluded and unspoiled white sands can be found along the incredible 40 km (25 miles) of **Colva Beach**, which run immediately south of Dabolim Airport, right down to the lovely and inviting **Benaulim** and **Betul**.

Velha Goa

The 16th-century churches to be found in Velha (Old) Goa have been beautifully restored, but you will doubtlessly notice that without the town buildings that used to surround them, they have acquired the strangely melancholic air of old museum-pieces. The town once had a population of 350,000 and some 100 churches. Nowadays the laterite stonework of many of the remaining churches has been thoughtfully and carefully covered with lime plaster to protect them against deterioration from the heavy waters of the dreaded Indian monsoons.

Distinguished from others by the harmonious simplicity of its ribvaulted nave, **St. Francis of Assisi** is the oldest church still standing in Velha Goa, perhaps dating as far back as 1521. The fine arabesque and floral frescoes are the work of local Indian artists who excelled at the themes wholly familiar to them—this in contrast with their efforts to paint portraits of the saints, with whose images they were, despite the hard work of the missionaries, perhaps not as much at home.

The Tuscan Renaissance façade of **Sé Cathedral**, the single biggest Christian church in India, has a certain elegance to it, despite a loss of symmetry when its north tower collapsed in 1776. The enormous main altar, which is dedicated to St. Catherine of Alexandria, shows some scenes from the saint's martyrdom in a series of sumptuously gilded panels.

Sandstone and granite were the materials used to build the Baroque church of **Bom Jesus**, famous for its casket of St. Francis Xavier's relics in the mausoleum to the right of the altar. The mausoleum was designed in Florence, as a gift from the Grand Duke of Tuscany.

THE CENTER

Here, at the holy city of Varanasi and the Ganga, you touch the very soul of India—and its sensuality as well, in the many temples of Khajuraho. You can also escape the preoccupations of existence at the wildlife sanctuary of Kanha. However, a reminder of the historic reality of the Indian Mutiny at Lucknow is also ever-present.

Lucknow

As a logical stopover on your way to Varanasi (coming from Delhi or from Calcutta), Lucknow is worth a visit for its special place in the history of India's determined fight for Independence—a focus of the Mutiny of 1857 (see pages 45–47).

The **British Residency**—today preserved as a monument—initially commemorated British resistance, but since Independence it

Each morning as the sun rises on the banks of the Ganga, the faithful come to pray.

has been visited by Indians interested in this relic of their own struggle for self-assertion, or interested in a family picnic on the lawns.

On a lawn surrounded by 24 palm trees, a cenotaph pays tribute to Chief Commissioner Sir Henry Lawrence, who was killed during the attack. An obelisk here honors "Native Officers and Sepoys, who died…nobly performing their duty." Indians comprised half the 1,600 troops defending the Residency. A little **museum** inside illustrates the history of the siege, with a model of the first Residency as well as rusty cannons and cannonballs, and prints, photos, and letters.

Down by the river, a short walk away, is the **Martyrs' Memorial**, inaugurated in 1957 on the centenary of the Mutiny to honor those who fought for India's independence.

Lucknow, with its 18th- and 19th-century mosques, used to be a Muslim stronghold; although the size of its community has now dwindled to only 30 percent of the country's population, it is one of the two single most important Indian centers of Shiite doctrine, the other being Mumbai.

Varanasi

One thing is certain: you cannot begin to fathom the mystery of India without a visit to Varanasi. Not that this old city will "explain" everything—in fact, its dramatic confrontations of life and death on the Ganga river, and of scholarship and superstition, may only mystify you even further—but the city's aura of sanctity is so overwhelming that it supercedes any need for rational explanations. Perhaps the Muslim conquerors once perceived the Hindus' reverence for Varanasi as a threat—there is no temple in this 3,000-year-old city dating from before the 18th century—but later it became a holy city for Muslims, too, with Emperor Aurangzeb even trying to rename it Muhammadabad.

The name Varanasi, misheard by Europeans as Benares, is derived from its site between the tributaries of the life-giving holy river Ganga, the Varuna and the Asi. Shiva is said to have poured the river down on the plains from the Himalayas; this mythical story leads Hindus to believe that Varanasi is the oldest city in the world.

Spots, Sacred and Secular

With the aid of a small mirror and a graceful arching hand gesture consecrated in temple sculpture all over India, pilgrims use white paste to daub a tilak, or tika, mark on their forehead, made up of a dot, stripes, or triangles, which denote their sect according to whether they are devotees of Vishnu or Shiva.

Women apply red ochre to a parting in their hair to denote their married status. These days many Indian women, whether married or unmarried, wear a spot in the center of the forehead called a bindi in any color, simply as a cosmetic accessory.

Probably founded by the Indo-Aryans around 1000 B.C., the city was established from earliest times as a famous seat of learning for Hindu thinkers, theologians, philosophers, and poets alike. It has remained ever since a center of the Hindu sciences. It was just outside Varanasi that Buddha's disciples gathered in the sixth century B.C. to hear his sermon at the Deer Park of Sarnath. Since then, Jain monks, Muslims, and Sikhs have proclaimed it a holy city, building monasteries, mosques, and temples here.

☞ The Ghats

The stone-stepped embankments leading down to the Ganga river are the gathering place of more than 250,000 pilgrims a year. To see the day unfold at the Ghats, you must rise before dawn to join the pilgrims. Holy men and women are up and about, busily chanting *"Ganga Mai ki jai!"*— "Praise be to Mother Ganga!"

Some are *sannyasi*, wandering beggars who have abandoned their homes and walked from as far as Chennai (Madras) to stand on the Ghats and pray, to bathe and drink the waters of the holy river, or just to sit and meditate on this supreme moment of their religious lives. Even the most aged and infirm travel here to die, for nothing is more blessed for

Families bring their dead to be cremated in a ceremony on the holiest of the Varanasi ghats.

a devout Hindu than to die in the great waters of the Varanasi and thus be released from the eternal cycle of rebirth.

Practically all roads in town lead down to the **Dasaswamedh Ghat**, where Brahma the Creator is said to have made a ritual sacrifice of 10 horses. At the top of the steps, holy men sit under their bamboo umbrellas chanting *mantras* and offering, for a coin or grains of rice, either sandalwood paste, flowers, or water from the Ganga.

At the water's edge, you can rent a boat and go into midstream for a view of the impressive skyline, which features many Hindu temples, gopuram towers, Muslim minarets, and Mughal domes. In the 5 km (3 miles) between her tributaries, the Ganga inscribes a crescent, turning north, as it is suggested, for one last gesture of farewell to her sacred home in the Himalayas before descending east towards the Bay of

Here, saris are stretched like bright ribbons to dry in the sun after being washed in the Ganga.

Bengal. You can ask your boatman to take you further upstream to the **Asi Ghat** before doubling back as far as the Panchganga.

Notice how the ritual ablutions, which are highly elaborate when performed by a learned Brahman, usually involve a kind of crouching movement completed at least three times in the water. Women, you will notice, bathe in full sari. You'll see plenty of soap and shampoo and, on the **Dhobi Ghat**, laundry-washing, too. After all, Mother Ganga, however sacred, is also just a river. Out on stone platforms, young men perform gymnastics, part of a devout self-discipline known as *danda*.

Those people who might at first be reluctant to confront the omnipresence of death along the river will be impressed by the simple dignity of the funeral rites here. Families bring their dead for their cremation to the holiest of Varanasi ghats, **Manikarnika**. The body, in a white shroud, is carried on a bier of bamboo to the river's edge, where a few drops of Ganga water are poured into the lips of the dead. The body is placed on a pyre of perfumed sandalwood, which is then set alight.

Jai Singh's observatory and learning temple, the **Scindia Ghat**, is at **Man Mandir Ghat**. The Alamgir Mosque rises behind the sacred **Panchganga Ghat**, said to be the mythical confluence of four Ganga subterranean tributaries.

The Town

The **Chawk** (bazaar) is famous for its perfumes, silks, and brassware. Look out for the gilded **Golden Temple of Vishwanath**, the holiest temple of Varanasi, forbidden to non-Hindus. You can view it from the building opposite before going behind the temple to see the sacred bull, stained deep vermilion by the libations of its worshippers.

Not By Faith Alone

It is hard to convince the faithful that the Ganga river is not pure. For centuries, those bodies not permitted for religious reasons to be cremated on the ghats—including babies and victims of cholera—have been dropped in the river while people bathe in and drink the water nearby.

Many firmly believe that the Ganga grants self-purification, which is reinforced for some by chemical analysis revealing a 0.05 percent sulphur content to conquer the bacteria. While faith has provided many bathers with a strong psychosomatic weapon against contamination, many of the people living permanently by the Varanasi ghats suffer from gastrointestinal diseases.

To combat Ganga's pollution as a result of dead bodies, sewage, and raw industrial waste, a $250 million campaign is finally under way. For the Indian government, faith needs a little help.

The Varanasi Hindu University has an **Art Museum** with a superb collection of 16th-century Mughal miniatures, considered superior to the national collection in Delhi.

Sarnath

Now a suburb of Varanasi, which is located about 10 km (6 miles) out of town, Sarnath is where Buddha gave his famous Deer Park sermon (the veritable foundation of the religion) to five disciples around the year 530 B.C. (see pages 19–21).

It quickly became a leading pilgrimage site, attracting devout Buddhists from many Eastern regions including Japan, China, and Southeast Asia as it still does today. Emperor Ashoka commanded his edict-pillars to be built within the monasteries and stupas, of which he had thousands constructed. But just like Varanasi, Sarnath suffered at the hands of Qutb-ud-din in the year 1194. Today the ruins have been well restored; they are accompanied by an excellent museum of Buddhist sculpture, which you should save to enjoy until last.

On the western side of the road coming out of Varanasi, you'll find the **Chaukhaudi Stupa**, built by a Gupta king in the fifth century A.D. With a proud octagonal tower that rises out of the top of the structure, it was built to mark the passage of the Emperor Humayun after his defeat in the 1540s. The remains of seven red-brick **monasteries** dating from the third century B.C. to the ninth century can be discerned among the ruins in a pretty setting of flowers and sacred neem trees. Since its attractive bricks were carried off to build houses in the town, only a platform of the **Main Shrine**, which once marked Buddha's dwelling place during his stay at Sarnath, remains.

West of the shrine, surrounded by an iron railing, are the stump and fragments of **Ashoka's Pillar**, which was once over 15 m (48 ft) high. Notice how the shine of the granite has withstood the elements for over 2,200 years. Its inscription warns the Indian people against the dissidence that could upset the important national unity under his leadership: "No one shall cause division in the Order of Monks."

The dominant feature of these ruins is the 45-m- (146-ft-) high, cylindrical **Dhamekh Stupa**, built in the fifth century A.D., which is believed by many to mark the ancient site of Buddha's most famous sermon.

Immediately below eight empty niches—perhaps they once held statues on display in the museum—is a beautiful frieze of fine floral and geometrical patterns interspersed with pretty birds and small seated Buddhas. If you should have a pair of binoculars, they will come in handy here: take a close look at the fine craftsmanship in this work of art.

Visitors will take delight in the **Museum**, which is a treasure-trove of superb early Indian sculpture dating from the third century B.C. to the fifth century A.D. Greeting you as you enter the museum is its famous masterpiece, the **lion-capital** of Ashoka's pillar, a high point of the distinctive art of the Mauryan empire. The lion, symbol of power and pride, was an understandable choice as the emblem of India's regained nationhood in 1947. Four vigorous lions stand back to back atop a frieze of animals comprising a horse, an elephant, a bull, and a smaller lion, each of them separated by a Wheel of Law, resting on the inverted lotus that once connected it to the pillar. Against the wall is the **Wheel of Law** that originally rose above the lions. As a gentle counterpoint to this, and sculpted some 700 years later, a **cross-legged Buddha** with a finely chiselled halo was added; look out for it. The Deer Park to the north of the excavations is just a modern afterthought, pleasant to relax in, but not related to the original.

Khajuraho

This town is famous for the erotic sculptures of its medieval Hindu temples; many come expecting to snigger. They leave, however, full of admiration, because the sandstone temples are marvels of harmony and the sculptures' true grace in their sensuality stifles any temptation to smirk.

We have British hunters to thank for uncovering these masterpieces, around 1840, half-buried in earth and hidden by the overgrown jungle. They didn't see the light of day until their excavation in 1923, 600 years after being abandoned during the Muslim conquests.

Khajuraho was capital of the Rajput kingdom of the Chandellas, a clan that brought vigour to love and war, as is clear in the temples they built from the tenth to the 12th centuries. The temples are divided into three groups: western, eastern, and southern. The major ones, in the western group, are in a beautifully kept park with paths leading easily from one to the other. To see the sculptures at their best, go in the morning or afternoon, or both, and then go back at night, when the temples are illuminated.

The lovely **Lakshmana** temple, dedicated to Vishnu, is one of the earliest, and the only one in which each of the four shrines (at each corner of the square platform on which it stands) are preserved.

Four *sikhara* domes rise above the entrance-porch in addition to: the mandapa hall for worshippers; a larger hall for dancing-girls; and the inner sanctuary, surrounded by an ambulatory for walking around the image of the deity. The silhouette seems to suggest the Himalayan home of the gods, but this may be more of a Brahmanic interpretation than the conception of the architect. The sculptures portray not only erotic postures, but also the adventures of Krishna: in one he uses all four arms to fend off two wrestlers.

Visvanartha, built in 1002, is more compact and ultimately more harmonious than Lakshmana. Its sculptures include a flute-playing maiden and a small nymph pulling a thorn from her foot.

The most spectacular temple of the western group is **Kandariya-Mahadeva**, with three domes culminating in the great 30-m- (98-ft-) high sikhara, composed of row upon row of 84 other, smaller sikharas.

Created at the height of the Chandellas' power in the mid-11th century, the sculpture inside is the most sophisticated and ingenious: *apsara* dancing-girls and *sura-sundari* nymphs coquettishly yawn-

Khajuraho is best known for the erotic sculpture that graces its lovely 10th-, 11th-, and 12th-century temples.

ing, scratching, applying their makeup, or playing with monkeys, parakeets, or with their cheerful lovers. The Kandariya is the largest of all the Khajuraho temples and adds, with its grand scale, a special exuberance to the life-enhancing spirit of the place.

The eastern group of structures includes three Jain temples. The most important is the tenth-century **Parsvanatha**, built in the classical Hindu sikhara-domed style and incorporating the sculptural themes of the Vishnu temples. While the religion of the Jains prohibits anything too explicit in sexuality, the ambience of Khajuraho is clearly contagious, and there are a lot of voluptuous, full-breasted ladies here that you don't usually see on a Jain temple.

Kanha

Kanha is famous, widely acknowledged as the best place for seeing an Indian tiger in the wild. In fact, for the sheer abundance of wildlife to be seen, Kanha is probably the best national park in India and should not be missed.

You might think the journey is a little complicated, but if you go to the trouble you will find it well worth the effort. You can either fly into Nagpur or, if you're coming from Khajuraho, take a train to Jabalpur and continue by road. It is, however, best to reserve your accommodation in forest rest-houses in advance of your journey.

The best season is February to May, when you'll be able to see plenty of beautiful cheetal (spotted deer), blackbuck, sloth bear, gaur or bison (largest of the wild cattle), wild boar, Kanha's unique barasingha ("12-pointer") swamp deer, and also monkeys galore.

The "Project Tiger" campaign is doing a sterling job here to protect the king of India's jungles without neglecting the elusive leopard. Enthusiastic bird-watchers might also spot black ibis and the crested serpent-eagle.

Tracking down the tiger is a subtle affair, and requires a degree of dedication, calm, and stealth. On the first morning, you take a jeep-safari at dawn to scout the terrain. The forest of sal trees and bamboo is a truly sweet-smelling delight, interspersed with rolling green meadows where the deer and gaur graze. Game-trackers will be out by this time in an attempt to locate the tiger's hunting ground for the evening safari.

A team of jungle-wise *mahouts* with elephants set out in the afternoon to seek the tiger in the most likely areas; you will be following in a jeep, keeping a watch out for any tell-tale signs that the tiger is near. The things to listen and look out for could be any one, or perhaps several, of the following: the alarm bark of the deer, a noisy screech from the monkeys, and—the most telling sign of all—vultures waiting for the tiger to abandon the leftovers of what he caught for lunch. When the elephant has located a tiger, the mahout signals and you hop aboard his howdah to penetrate the jungle. *Et voilà!*

Sanchi

About one hour away from Bhopal, the stupas of Sanchi are the most admired Buddhist monuments in the whole of India. The site, from the third century B.C., when Emperor Ashoka ordered stupas containing the Buddha's relics to be built, is on a 91-m (300-ft) hill on the Vindhya plateau.

An intricate detail from a torana gate, believed to protect the Buddhist stupas from evil sprits.

Stupas were originally burial mounds; Buddhists developed them into shrines of plaster-covered stone, inside which are caskets containing relics of Buddha. Crowned by a *chhattra* (umbrella) made of stone, the stupa was erected on a terrace with a fence to enclose the path. The stupas of Sanchi lay in the jungle until they were uncovered by the British in 1818, but delay in their restoration led to their plunder. Three stupas and the temples and monasteries from the fifth to the 12th century A.D. can still be seen.

The **Great Stupa**, Stupa I, built in the first century B.C., envelops a smaller mound erected some 200 years earlier. It is surrounded by stone railings; in the terrace railing are four *torana* gates, off north–south and east–west axes, perhaps in order to deceive evil

The stupas in Sanchi were plundered early last century, but there is still much here to admire.

spirits. Formed by square posts with finely sculptured panels, the gates are topped by three architraves (crossbars), one placed above the other with dwarfs or animals.

At the time Stupa I was built, Buddha himself was not represented in human form, but symbolized by the horse on which he rode away from his palace, by the wheel of law, by his footprints, and by the pipal tree under which he found enlightenment.

The rest of humanity is present in the form of his worshippers, his adversaries, dancers, and *yaksi* nymphs. Despite the strict asceticism preached through Buddhism, it's clear that the craftsmen employed were given free rein regarding their joyous sensuality.

The smaller **Stupa III**, to the northeast of the Great Stupa, has one torana gate; it was originally built to contain the relics of the two disciples of Buddha, which are preserved in a casket with pieces of bone and jewels. The **Stupa II** mound is down on the western slope of the hill. Its circular balustrade has four L-shaped entrances with a simpler decoration of flora, fauna, and Buddha symbols. Historians have noted that the horsemen are using stirrups, the earliest known example of their use in India.

THE EAST

The east of India encompasses the birthplace of Buddhism at Bodh

Gaya, the great Hindu temples of Bhubaneshwar, and the challenge of Calcutta, a huge confrontation of vitality and hardship. You can cool off in the green tea plantations of Darjeeling or in the mountains of Sikkim.

Calcutta

The town's reputation for squalor has so deeply imbedded itself in the world's imagination that it comes as a surprise to find the Calcuttans to be the liveliest bunch of people in

Calcutta teems with its 10 million citizens, an active and thriving modern Indian city.

the country. Bengalis are irrepressible; perhaps the challenge of coping with daily life in this city of 10 million has sharpened their wit.

Survival here is a creative art; it is no accident that Calcutta remained the country's intellectual and cultural capital long after it relinquished government to Delhi. Calcutta was the home of the writer Rabindranath Tagore, India's first Nobel Prize winner, and of the philosophers Ramakrishna and Vivekananda. Creative people still make their name here.

After the establishment-minded press of Delhi, the newspapers in Calcutta seem bright, ebullient, and vitriolic; while Mumbai's filmmakers are masters of melodrama, Calcutta's cinema is known for its sensitivity and poetry, producing faithful mirrors of village and city life in the hands of such directors as Satyajit Ray and Mrinal Sen. It is the proper home for the country's best museum, which is simply and aptly named "the Indian Museum."

For all their ardent nationalism, Calcuttans retain a strong, if sometimes sardonic, attachment to things British; in particular they have an affection for the English language, which you'll find spoken here with the most British of accents—and often with a good deal more style and elegance than the British themselves can muster.

The West Bank

Even if you're not arriving in the city by train, start your visit at **Howrah Station**. The crowds in and around the station will douse you in something of a baptism by fire; you'll soon realize that only a small

Toehold on the Hooghly

When the body of Shiva's wife, Kali, was dismembered after her death, the little toe of her right foot fell onto the bank of the Hooghly river—that's where the village of Kalikata grew up. Together with the villages of Sutanuti and Govindpur, it was sold to the East India Company in the 1690s to set up the trading center of Calcutta.

It was the Nawab of Bengal's attack on the British settlement in 1756 that brought Robert Clive's crushing reprisal at Plassey and the consolidation of the British Empire in India. Calcutta, with its port connection to east Asia and subsequent development of its jute, cotton, silk, and tea industries, remained its capital for the next 150 years. The Bengalis and Calcuttans in particular were trouble-makers, however, violently stirred by the growing nationalism. The British found it wise to move the political capital to Delhi in 1911.

Ever since Independence, when Partition cut Calcutta's jute and other industries off from their natural hinterland in eastern Bengal, the city has suffered many economic difficulties, compounded by a huge influx of refugees from Bangladesh. The town remains a hotbed of active, radical politics, and a stronghold of the Indian Communist Party.

fraction of them are actually there to take a train. The station is a home for many: its entrance hall and platforms are dormitory and kitchen.

Head next for the restful **Botanical Gardens**, laid out in the 18th century, boasting 35,000 species of flowers and shrubs. The first tea cuttings were brought to these gardens from China to found the plantations of Darjeeling (see page 158) and Assam. The gardens' pride is a 200-year-old banyan tree, the *Ficus bengalensis*, or strangling fig tree. Some fungus destroyed its central trunk, but it still thrives, having aerial roots and a circumference of 400 m (1,300 ft).

The **Howrah Bridge**, itself a national monument, conveys you across the river to the city center. This massive steel suspension bridge stages the most magnificent traffic jams; it is a great place to gauge the Bengali temperament.

The City

Another park, the **Maidan**, is in the center of the city; landscaped to allow for a clear line of fire from all around **Fort William**, it was rebuilt by Robert Clive on a more easily defended site than its predecessor. Like Britain's Hyde Park, the Maidan attracts ferocious soapbox orators predicting the end of the world, but it

Calcutta offers a daily riot of traffic and people along with its many noteworthy sites.

is also visited by the most wonderful charlatans peddling medicine and other questionable substances.

The **Ochterlony Monument**—originally named after an obscure British warrior—is one of many Calcutta landmarks which has not exactly taken on its new name (Shahid Minar). It is the focus of the city's boisterous political rallies. **Eden Gardens**, with pond and pagoda and the venerable Calcutta cricket grounds, are by the river.

The **Victoria Memorial** offers a history of the bygone Raj, Anglo-Renaissance in style with a touch of Mughal influence. Its white marble was brought from the Rajasthani quarries used for building the Taj Mahal. Commissioned by Viceroy Lord Curzon, it was paid for by "voluntary contributions" from the maharajas and nawabs.

Catch up on the Indian avant-garde—and the bohemian people of Calcutta—at the **Academy of Fine Arts** on the southeast corner of the Maidan.

Running along the eastern edge of the Maidan, the **Chowringhee Road** (Nehru Road) marks the old European neighborhood whose mansions once won Calcutta the wishful name of "City of Palaces." These days it is a busy shopping street with big hotels and cinemas, gigantic film billboards featuring actresses in wet saris, and a roadway that is so chock-a-block with cows, rickshaws, pedestrians, and bicycles that cars are often seen going backwards.

The **Indian Museum**, by Chowringhee and Sudder Street, makes an excellent home for art treasures from the ancient Maurya and Gupta eras which had been disintegrating after centuries of exposure to the merciless natural elements. The great Buddhist carvings on the railings from the Bharhut stupa (second century B.C.), comparable to those of Sanchi (see page 143), are preserved in the **Bharhut Gallery**. The **Gandhara Room** displays the earliest sculptures representing Buddha in human form (first century A.D.).

Dalhousie Square (also called BBD Bagh), on the site of the original Fort William north of the Maidan, was once the center of Britain's imperial bureaucracy. Here, scribblers of the East India Company—*babus* to friend and foe—duplicated and triplicated everything they could lay their hands on in the Writers' Buildings. It now serves just the Government of West Bengal, but with an undiminished number of babus.

It takes a detective to find the original site of the **Black Hole** at the domed General Post Office on the west side of Dalhousie Square, since most Indians aren't interested in helping you. They generally see the incident (see pages 43–44) as having been a piece of elaborate British propaganda thought up to justify Clive's retaliation. A plaque marks the spot in an arch at the northeast corner of the post office.

This Jain temple seems like an ancient oasis of tranquility set down in the middle of modern Calcutta.

Most of the major British Indian buildings prior to the 20th century were built not by an architect but by a soldier-engineer copying existing plans of buildings back home. The magnificent **Raj Bhavan** (Governor's Residence), which you can find due north of the Maidan, copied famous Kedleston Hall in Derbyshire. The nearby **St. John's Church**, Calcutta's first cathedral, is an Indian version of London's St. Martin-in-the-Fields; look in the south aisle for John Zoffany's amusing painting of *The Last Supper*. Zoffany used the East India Company men as models, with the painter's sworn enemy, Mr. Paull, as Judas. The tomb of Job Charnock, the Company official who founded the city of Calcutta, is in the church cemetery.

The **Marble Palace**, a bizarre tribute to Western art and architecture, can be found on tiny Muktaram Babu Street northeast of Dalhousie Square. Built by the hugely wealthy land-owning family of Raja Majendra Mullick Bahadur, this huge Palladian villa-turned-museum has a park and menagerie of exotic birds. It recalls William Randolph Hearst's castle in California, with its imaginative juxtaposition of ancient Roman and Chinese sculpture, fine Venetian glass chandeliers, Sèvres porcelain, old Flemish masters, and naughty French erotica. The odd Mullick still hangs around to play Chopin in the ballroom or billiards in the parlor.

Like their European counterparts, Indian gypsies bedeck themselves in striking jewelry.

Bhubaneshwar

As you fly down the coast from Calcutta, you'll suddenly spot a small forest of tall domes in a town with a lake at its center. These are the temples of that most holy city, Bhubaneshwar.

The capital of Orissa is a center for easy day-trips to the ancient Jain cave monasteries of Udaigiri, the chariot-temple of Konark, and the sacred pilgrimage town of Puri. Once there were thousands of Hindu and Jain sanctuaries in and around Bhubaneshwar. Some 500, mostly ruins, can still be traced, but only 30 are visitable. Three or four are masterpieces of Hindu architecture.

The oldest temples, dating from the seventh and eighth centuries, are grouped around the sacred "Ocean Drop" lake of **Bindu Sagar**, the focus for bathing and purification ceremonies before the annual festivals. East of the Bindu Sagar, the tenth-century **Muktesvara**, is a rust-colored stone temple dedicated to Shiva, with a small bathing

Wheel of Life

Jagannath, the Universal Lord, is an incarnation of Vishnu the Preserver, offering Hindus of all castes the opportunity to escape the torment of perpetual rebirth. Thousands of pilgrims congregate at Puri all year round, but mostly for the June/July festival when the three great wooden chariots of Jagannath, his brother, and his sister are drawn through the streets. Then, the faithful can liberate themselves by touching the crudely carved wooden deities, models of which are sold in the town.

Although orthodox followers of Vishnu insist that Jagannath is a life-giving force, the belief still persists that the frenzied activity of the festival has led some to seek ultimate release by hurling themselves under the huge wheels of Jagannath's chariot, whence the English word "juggernaut," which means a great force demanding utter self-sacrifice.

tank and gracefully arched torana gate. There is great peace and dignity in the temple's proportions; the low curved pyramid on the hall of worship and ribbed sikhara dome over the sanctum repeat the classic silhouette of Orissa temples.

The **Rajarani**, standing on a platform at the end of a pleasant garden, is a more robust structure than that of the Muktesvara, with a more pronounced pyramid over the worship hall, and a powerful sikhara behind it.

The greatest of the city's many temples is the late-11th-century **Lingaraja**, south of the Bindu Sagar. Off limits to non-Hindus, it can be viewed from an observation platform specially erected for the purpose by Lord Curzon. A pair of binoculars will be particularly useful here, in order to appreciate the splendid detail of the carving on the soaring central tower dominating a whole complex of temples. It is dedicated to the Lord of the Three Worlds, Tribhuvanesvara, who gave the town of Bhubaneshwar its modern day name.

Udaigiri

The cave monasteries of Udaigiri are close to Bhubaneshwar airport. Excavated from a sandstone hill in the third and second centuries B.C., the Udaigiri (Sunrise Hill) caves were dwellings for priests and monks when Jainism was the state religion in the kingdom of Kalinga.

Rani's Monastery (Cave 1) has carvings of elephants, maidens, and court dancers, but unlike the caves of Ajanta and Ellora (see page 115), there are no temples or central halls for worship.

Further up the hill, **Ganesha Gumpha** (Cave 10) is set back on an esplanade and guarded by two sturdy stone elephants holding branches of mangoes. The friezes are more sophisticated, showing

archers riding elephants and a king of Kalinga reclining with his queen. Cave 14, **Hathi Gumpha** (Elephant Cave), is important for the inscription above the entrance, which details the conquests and irrigation projects completed during King Kharavela's 13-year reign, around 50 B.C.

Konark

The **Sun Temple** of Konark was conceived as a gigantic chariot

The Sun Temple in Konark, though it may look as if it could roll off at any minute, has stood still since the 13th century.

Another elaborate chariot—though this one carries men, not gods—located in Konark.

for the great sun-god Surya cantering inland from the Indian Ocean. The sikhara that once towered 60 m (200 ft) into the air like some symbolic and divine charioteer has gone, but the grandiose pyramid of the **Jagmohan** (Hall of Audience), where the priests used to officiate, still soars above 12 pairs of huge stone wheels sculpted into its huge platform and drawn by numerous galloping horses. The temple was built in the 13th century, but the sikhara toppled, its porous stone ruined by storms and plunderers—and by the ambitious concept of its architect. As you climb over the remains, you'll find they have a decidedly secular air. Surya was given his due with dignified green chlorite statues of *parsva-devatas* (sun-deities) set in niches facing the four points of the compass, and much of the sculpture profusely decorating the walls emphasizes his life as a king—his battles, the royal hunt, and life at court. The sensuality of the aristocratic lovers recalls Khajuraho (see page 139).

The wheels of the chariot themselves, symbols of the Hindu cycle of rebirth, have beautifully carved spokes and hubs decorated with kings and gods. Beneath the wheels, there are lively carved friezes of elephants playing with children. Look out as well for a giraffe, which indicates the Indian west coast's early contact with Africa. The masterpieces among the free-standing statuary, though, are the war-horses trampling the king's enemies and the splendid elephants crushing the demons.

European sailors, for whom the temple was an important landmark, enabling them to keep out of the dangerous shallows of the Orissa coast (they nearly had it turned into a lighthouse), called it the Black Pagoda—in order to be able to distinguish it from the "White Pagoda" of Puri's whitewashed Jagganath Temple further down the coast. After the huge sikhara tower had collapsed, however, the British saved the pyramidal Jagmohan by pouring concrete into its core; now the Archaeological Survey of India is heroically performing massive restoration work on the important sculpture.

Puri

Even if you can't be in Puri for the tremendous Rath Yatra Festival in June/July, the town is worth a visit just to see a community devoted almost entirely to the "industry" of its great **Temple of Jaggannath**, either directly or by trading with the pilgrims.

Non-Hindus are not permitted within the temple precincts, but you can get a good **view** from the roof of the Raghunandan Library near the temple wall. Some 6,000 priests, artisans, and other workers are employed within the grounds. Of the four main buildings, all of them whitewashed and decorated with bright painted sculptures, the first is where the worshippers bring offerings of flowers and fruit, the second is for sacred dances, and the third for viewing the divine effigies, which are enshrined in the sanctum of the fourth and tallest edifice.

Puri also has a beautiful **beach**, southwest of town, which is ideal for cooling off—but those aren't sandcastles the Indians are making, they're miniature temples, for this is the **Swarga Dwara** (Heaven's Gateway), where the faithful wash away their sins.

Darjeeling

Before you overdose on the countless temples or even just on the heat of the plains, follow the wise example of the long-gone British of Calcutta and get up into the hills and greenery which lead to the lush cool of the celebrated Darjeeling tea gardens.

At 2,185 m (7,100 ft), it's a bit hard to breathe in the rarefied air, but take in the splendor of the Himalayan mountains—mount Kanchenjunga situated in Sikkim (see page 162), and, if you're lucky on a clear day in April and May or in late September and October, Mount Everest itself, up in Nepal.

In the year 1835, the raja of the then-independent kingdom of Sikkim was pressured into ceding Darjeeling to the British. The Brits believed it would be a healthy place for soldiers and East India Company employees to recover from the ills of the plains, but above all they found the area strategically useful for controlling a pass into much-contested Nepal. With tea from seeds smuggled out of China and an influx of plantation labor from Nepal, the little village of 100 souls grew to a community of 10,000 by 1849. Now Darjeeling is part of West Bengal, but Nepali remains the official language and most residents are of Nepalese and Tibetan origin. Buddhists account

for 18 percent of the population.

A major part of the pleasure of Darjeeling is in getting here. Although you're driving along narrow mountain roads, you'll feel much safer than in the plains, because everyone takes infinitely more care; lorry and bus drivers are clearly subdued by the deep ravines.

But the best way to travel up —at least part of the way, if you're too impatient to take 6 hours for the whole 80 km (50

India shares its tallest mountain, Kanchenjunga, with its neighbor Nepal.

☞ miles)—is by the **Darjeeling Himalayan Railway**, more popularly and humorously known as the "Toy Train," which starts out at
Siliguri, not far from Bagdogra. Built in 1881, the tiny steam-train
on a 60-cm (2-ft) track climbs, loops, and zigzags through dense
forests of sal, Chinese cedar, and teak which are alive with jungle
birds and mountain streams. Watch for Pagla Jhora, the Mad Tor-
rent, just after Gladstone's Rock (shaped like the statesman's head).
Also keep your eyes open for a first view of Kanchenjunga, 8,586 m
(28,168 ft) high and the world's third highest peak, after Mount
Everest and Pakistan's K2.

The railway builders admitted it might have been safer to dig
some tunnels, but they preferred to go "round the mountain" to
allow for a better view of the terraced tea gardens and the valleys
plunging down to the Bengal plains. Certainly when you reach the
railway's high point, 2,257 m (7,407 ft), at **Ghoom**, the view as
you hover out on the loop over Darjeeling is in every sense of the
word breathtaking.

The only relics of the British Raj are the (now) all-Indian, and
still very private, Darjeeling Club, and a couple of tea rooms and Edwardian hotels such as the Windermere (with coal-burning fires and
☞ hot water bottles at night). The real British legacy is in the **tea gardens**, all Indian-run, which offer a beautiful green setting for the
town and insight into tea growing and processing methods (see page
218). Makaibari and Happy Valley are among those open for visitors
without obligation to buy. Your hotel will book for you.

A drive to **Tiger Hill** before dawn is a popular excursion which
Indians and Westerners go on for different reasons, though both
show the same almost religious excitement as the night fades. From
an observation platform, you can get a terrific view, away to the
north, of Mount Kanchenjunga and, on a good day, just a small

*Terraced tea gardens cascade down toward the Bengal plains
from the Darjeeling Himalayan Railway tracks.*

jagged peak in the distance — yes, Mount Everest. But you'll notice the Indians are facing east. What matters is not the rare opportunity of seeing the world's tallest mountain, but seeing the *sunrise*.

For a closer look at the true roof of the world, consider a seven-day camping trek, on foot or pony, to **Sandakhpu** (3,650 m/11,700 ft). You'll get better views of Mount Kanchenjunga and Mount Everest and pass through lovely forests of chestnut, magnolia, and rhododendron. During April and May, the orchids will be in bloom.

Armchair mountaineers invariably enjoy the excellent museum at the **Himalayan Mountaineering Institute** in Darjeeling. It has on display some fascinating memorabilia of Himalayan expeditions, in particular the equipment used by local Sherpa Tensing Norgay (here Indianized as Shri Tensingh), when, with Edmund Hillary, he was the first to conquer Everest in 1953.

Sikkim

Once again, a great part of the joy of the place is the journey itself, by road to the capital, **Gangtok** (1,768 m/5,800 ft), in eastern Sikkim

---

Permits for Darjeeling and Sikkim

Being so close to the militarily sensitive border areas of Chinese Tibet, both Darjeeling and Sikkim require entry permits (free). Darjeeling is easy: either you obtain it automatically at the Indian Embassy at home when you get your visa or, if you're flying to Bagdogra, the closest airport, your passport will be stamped right there. You'll need a special permit for trekking beyond Darjeeling, but it's no trouble.

A permit for Sikkim, extendible for a limited period, should be requested via an Indian Embassy at least four weeks prior to your departure from home, and picked up at the Deputy Commissioner's Office in Darjeeling. In theory the permits are also issued at the Ministry of Home Affairs in Delhi, but the red tape is formidable.

through the most spectacular scenery: rivers roaring through gorges, deep valleys outlined by terraced rice paddies, and forested hills. To protect India's border with China and put an end to the unrest over the Raja's autocratic rule, the region of Sikkim was incorporated into the Indian Union in 1975. The people of Sikkim are mostly made up of Nepalese and Lepchas—the country's original settlers known also as Rongpan, the people of the ravines—and Bhutias from Tibet.

The colorful Tibetan Buddhist monasteries are the most attractive sight in the valleys near Gangtok. The most easily accessible of them is **Rumtek**, built in 1968 after China drove the maroon-robed Tibetan monks of the Karmapa sect into exile. Other, older monasteries from the 18th century, based

A Mauryan sculpture from the Patna Museum, which holds many other treasures as well.

150 km (92 miles) west of Gangtok at **Pemayangtse** and **Tashiding**, are well worth visiting, but access to them may be restricted at times by the military authorities.

Patna

The capital of Bihar serves as a base for visits to the sanctuaries of Bodh Gaya, Rajgir, and Nalanda, but its bazaars, first-class sculpture museum, a major Sikh temple, and the views of the Ganga river make it worth at least a day of your time.

Patna was already in existence 2,500 years ago, when Buddha and Mahavira were active here. It later became the capital of the Mauryan emperors, in the third century B.C., and one of the largest cities in the world at 3 km (2 miles) across and 12 km (7 miles) along the Ganga. The British used Patna for manufacturing and distributing opium in the 19th century, to keep China supplied with its favorite drug. The old warehouses can still be seen by the river in the Gulzarbagh district, now housing a printing press.

The **Golghar**, on the west side of town near the river, is evidence of the more altruistic side of British activity in Patna. This great flat-topped dome, a granary some 27 m (87 ft) high, was erected in 1786 by Captain John Garstin "for the perpetual prevention of famine," after the terrible famine of 1770. Climb to the top for a fine **view** of the town and river.

The open ground on the edge of the **Maidan** is where Mahatma Gandhi held mass prayer-meetings. Stand in the middle of the new **Ganga Bridge** to get a sense of the effect the river has on the lives of the Indians; it is 3 km (2 miles) wide here.

Har Mandir Takht in old Patna will give you a sense of the Sikh community. It was built on the birthplace of Gobind Singh (1666–1708), who called on the Sikhs to defend their faith with armed force (see pages 18–19). The well that served Gobind Singh's house is now a marble shrine. The sanctuary exemplifies piety and militancy. A priest will explain the faith and show you, among the guru's relics, his cradle, shoes, and weapons. Above the sanctuary, priests and neophytes chant from the scriptures of the *Adi Grant* in a hall, now a museum to history and a record of the tortures suffered by Sikhs. The **bazaar** nearby sells cheap bamboo and leather goods.

This towering structure is the Buddhist Mahabodhi Temple, built in the sixth century.

Patna Museum offers Mauryan sculpture: a stone yaksi (symbol of fertility), a maiden and Buddhas, a four-armed *Padmapani*, and a reclining *Avalokitesvara*.

Bodh Gaya

The site of the pipal tree or *bodhi*—the tree of wisdom where Gautama Siddhartha became the Enlightened One, Buddha—stands for one of the four great pilgrimages of his life. The others are those of his birth at Lumbini (Nepal); his first sermon at Sarnath (see page 138); and of his death at Kushinagar. The sanctuary is just outside Gaya, south of Patna.

E. M. Forster fans can undertake their own private pilgrimage 25 km (15 miles) north, to the Barabar Caves, which were the setting for the "Marabar incident" in Forster's famous novel *Passage to India*. As Forster commented, however, they have no artistic merit in themselves.

The towering structure of the **Mahabodhi Temple**, built in the sixth century, evokes the gopuram gateways of south India. In keep-

Waiting for Nirvana

The demons did not make it very easy for Gautama Siddhartha to achieve enlightenment. As he sat there beneath the pipal tree for 49 days, the demons played the age-old game of "good guy, bad guy" to distract him. First, they hit him with whirlwind, then tempest, flood, and earthquake. He just sat there. Then the devil Mara brought in his lovely daughters, Desire, Pleasure, and Passion, to seduce him with song, dance, and caresses. He just sat there. They offered to make him king of the world. He just continued to sit until they gave up and went away.

Buddha's ordeal was a godsend for Indian art. In early Buddhism, when it was considered sacrilegious to portray Buddha in human form, his torments and temptations provided sculptors with a rich alternative source to draw upon.

ing with other early Buddhist tenets, there is no figurative representation of Buddha here, However, there is a large gilded statue from a later period inside, and behind the temple are the spreading branches and trunks of the sacred **Bodhi Tree**, which is said to have grown from a sapling of the first one that stood here 2,500 years ago. Pilgrims visiting the temple reverently drape its branches with white and saffron-colored veils. A platform marks Buddha's seat and a set of large footprints symbolize his presence, while stone bowls mark where he walked. Hindus and Buddhists still bathe where he bathed. The **museum** has stupa railings, and the granite Buddhas date from the ninth century.

The university of Nalanda thrived in the seventh century, but was destroyed in the twelfth.

The importance of the Bodh Gaya pilgrimage is evident in the Japanese, Thai, Tibetan, Burmese, and Chinese temples nearby.

Rajgir

This ancient city is due northeast of Bodh Gaya, out on the road to Naland, and it has been holy to both the Buddhists and Jains since the sixth century B.C. As Rajagriha, the capital of the Magadha kingdom, the town was frequented at different times by both Buddha and his contemporary Vardhamana Mahavira, the founder of the Jain religion.

The surrounding green hills are topped by numerous temples of both religions, the best known being on **Gridhakuta** (Vulture's Peak), where Buddha is believed to have converted the once fierce Mauryan warrior king Bimbisara to the peaceful doctrine of non-violence. The Japanese have built a great white **stupa** on Rajgir's principle hill, which you can reach by aerial ropeway—a pleasant way to survey the rugged countryside.

Nalanda

In order for you to get the most out of the fascinating ruins of the great monastery and the University of Nalanda, it is recommended that you use the services of a guide from the Archaeological Survey of India.

In the third century B.C., Ashoka founded the first monastery in the town of Rajgir, which became a center of learning under the

Try Cambridge, It's Easier

According to Hiuen Tsang, the University in Nalanda had 1,500 teachers and 10,000 students, all on scholarships funded by the "endowment" of 100 villages in the area. But getting in was not a piece of cake.

Entrance examinations were exactly that: you couldn't get past the entrance of the university before answering a difficult oral question on philosophy, posed by the gatekeeper. Only ten percent got through the gate.

Gupta kings 600 years later. By the time the Chinese sage, Hiuen Tsang, came here in the seventh century, it was a thriving university for teaching philosophy, logic, grammar, medicine, and Buddhist theology. It also sent missionaries to spread Buddhism to Tibet and attracted scholars from China, Burma, Thailand, and Cambodia. It was destroyed by the Muslims at the end of the 12th century and the monks fled to Nepal and Tibet.

The **museum** has a good model of the original university and its monastery buildings, worth studying before you go out to the site. It also has a fine collection of bronzes from the ninth to the 12th centuries. On the **excavation site**, you will see remains of dormitories in addition to the refectory, kitchens, baths, lecture halls, libraries, and temples.

THE SOUTH

Travelling between Delhi, Mumbai, and Calcutta, it's easy to forget that southern India exists. The attitude of northern Indians tends to be rather disparaging towards it, but a tour of the peninsula reveals a bright and cheerful people with a culture as rich and varied as their greener landscapes—the beautiful Malabar and Coromandel coasts.

The Dravidians who make up most of the southern populations don't mind being seen as different from northerners, but they don't want to be disregarded. Archaeologists can trace their origins to the builders of the first cities, Harappa and Mohenjodaro, in the Indus valley. Their religion included elements of Hinduism such as Shiva's phallic lingam and his sacred bull, Nandi, *before* the Brahmanic Indo-Aryans arrived. Driven south, the Dravidians remained not only geographically separate, but also politically independent, impervious to the waves of foreign invaders.

Farmers labor in sight of Karnataka's granite hills, which look like the stone walls of some forgotten giant's garden.

Since Hindus battled Muslims until the end of the 16th century, they were by no means united. The Hoysalas of Karnataka, the Cheras of Kerala, the Cholas, Pandyas, and Pallavas of Tamil Nadu all fought among themselves until the kingdom of Vijayanagar (Hampi in Karnataka) emerged as dominant in the 14th century. Each of these kingdoms showed cultural vitality, exporting temple-builders together with their spices and ivory to Burma, Malaysia, Cambodia, and Java. Suffering less than the north from the ravages of Muslim iconoclasts, their temples have survived in profusion and in much better condition.

Bangalore is in the vanguard of India's modernization, and Chennai, though without the self-promotion of Mumbai, easily produces twice as many feature films as Mumbai.

Madurai, Thanjavur (Tanjore), Belur, and Halebid are custodians of the peninsula's ancient art treasures. The strong regional identity of the south has repeatedly foiled attempts to spread Hindi and make it the national language here. On the east coast they point out that Tamil literature is much richer than Hindi. On the west, the people of Kerala, who speak Malayalam, boast the highest literacy rate in the country: 90 percent for the whole State, compared with 81 percent for the next highest (the district of Mizoram); and this with a national average of just over 52 percent.

Much better served by the rains, with some parts benefitting from the peninsula's two monsoon seasons, in the summer and early winter, the south's vegetation is luxuriant and colorful. There are coconut groves on the Malabar west coast, palmyra palms on the Coromandel east, and in between, a more barren landscape of rugged mountains and dramatic rocky outcroppings, relieved here and there by a patch of "Flame of the Forest" trees, hibiscus, or deep green jungle, as well as plentiful trickling streams, lotus ponds, and lakes covered with scarlet lilies.

Bangalore

Modern and efficient, the capital of Karnataka is a convenient gateway to the western half of the peninsula.

Under the former British Raj, Bangalore, at an altitude of 930 m (3,000 feet), was the summer refuge for its Madras-based officials, who with their parks and greenery had made Bangalore the "garden city." The spectacular growth of India's boom town in electronics, aviation, telecommunications, and machine tools has noticeably changed the climate since the 1970s; it is several degrees hotter here now than it was thirty years ago. There are still pleasant walks to be had, however, in **Cubbon Park** and in the terraced greenery of the botanical gardens of **Lal Bagh**.

Bangalore-Mysore road is a delightful introduction to the verdant and pleasant land of the south. Leading you along tributary

streams of the Cauvery river, past groves of mango trees, sugar cane fields, and rice paddies, it is suddenly broken by the soaring mountain of solid granite which director David Lean made the location for the fateful picnic in his film of E. M. Forster's novel *Passage to India*. You can visit Srirangapatnam and Somnathpur (page 175) on the way.

Mysore

The home town of the maharajas regains a flicker of its old glory every October during the Dussehra festival, when the heir of the old rulers of Mysore State is paraded through the streets on his golden throne, surrounded by gorgeously caparisoned elephants (see page 209).

Mysore remains a pleasant, airy city, famous for its sandalwood and frangipani, jasmine, and musk. The maharaja's palace is a museum by day and

Dawn in Mysore offers a view of relics from the age of the maharajas, seen through a cool and pleasant mist.

Mysore is a lovely, fragrant city, scented with sandalwood and musk.

lit up at night. It was constructed in 1897 (after its predecessor was burned down, because the maharaja wanted a new one) and represents all the excesses of Mughal nostalgia and undigested Victoriana. Doors of solid silver open onto the multicolored, stylish décor of marble, mahogany, and ivory. The highlight is an art gallery, with paintings of the maharajas in very British, landed-gentry poses, and a glass case featuring a "rolled gold replica of the British crown" set between a tea kettle which is noticeably bigger than the coffee pot near it.

On the summit of the **Chamundi Hill**, the Sri Chamundeswari Temple offers a fine view of Mysore. On your way back down the hill, take a look at the massive black **Nandi** bull, Shiva's sacred mascot, with chains and bells that are a mixture of both real and sculpted items hung around its neck.

Another popular sight are the **Brindavan Gardens**, in Mughal style, some 19 km (12 miles) north of Mysore, worth visiting at night when the fountains are flood-lit.

Srirangapatnam

The names of many southern towns are longer than their main streets. Situated due east of Mysore, Srirangapatnam was the site of the battles against the Muslim ruler Tipu Sultan in the 1790s, in which the British gained control of the peninsula.

The fort, which was taken by Lord Cornwallis and Colonel Arthur Wellesley (the Iron Duke with the rubber boots), no longer stands today, but the sultan's summer palace, **Darya Daulat Bagh**, has been preserved and made into a museum honoring the brave resistance of Tipu and his father, Haidar Ali.

Somnathpur

The **Kesava Temple**, built in 1268, is a tiny, shining jewel in the crown of Indian architecture. The structure is small, no more than 10 m (30 ft) high, and its *vimanas* (shrines) are set on a low, modest platform, but the temple achieves a grandeur in miniature,

Diamonds Will Do It

If the great Mughal emperors turned to the ladies of their harems more for political intrigue and court ceremony than for sexual adventures, the Maharajas of Mysore did not have the same priorities. One of them learned from a Chinese scholar that powdered diamonds made an ideal aphrodisiac. The eager prince promptly crushed practically all his kingdom's stock of sparklers, but the ladies were not impressed. He had more success, however, when his favorite lady, horrified by this destruction of what, after all, are a girl's best friend, persuaded him to let her personally prepare the powdered potion.

peacefully enclosed in its courtyard and isolated from the rest of the village.

The temple has been dedicated to Vishnu in his various aspects: as Janardana the Punisher, shown as a rigid, solemn-looking statue on the north vimana; as Kesava the Radiant, after whom the temple is named but whose statue is missing from the central shrine; and as Venugopala, the Krishna on the south shrine, with another Krishna as cowherd listening at his feet.

With a domed sikhara on each shrine, the temple's overall effect remains "horizontal" in the style of the Hoysala kingdom, emphasized by the layers of narrow, parallel carved friezes running around the walls. Every square centimeter of the temple's surface is sculpted. An unusual feature in the Hoysala temples is that their carvings are signed by the sculptors.

Like the statues of Romanesque and Gothic cathedrals portraying events from the Bible, the carvings were intended to be read like a book by those who had no access to the scriptures, which were at that time reserved for the Brahmins. They tell the stories of the gods—of the mischievous tricks of Krishna, as a child stealing butter from his

Bright crops of sunflowers are cultivated in the fields surrounding Halebid.

mother and later as a young man stealing saris from girls bathing in the river—and of the adventures of the epic *Mahabharata*.

Belur and Halebid

The most comfortable way to see these important Hoysala temples is to visit them on either side of an overnight stay at Hassan, 120 km (75 miles) northwest of Mysore.

The **Chenna Kesava Temple** in Belur is also dedicated to Vishnu the Radiant, but it was built in 1117, 150 years before the Kesava. Legend has it that all Belur, Halebid, and Somnathpur temples designed by the same architect. The Belur temple's silhouette makes for

an unfinished look, but it's not certain that towers or domes were ever planned. Here too, it is the sculpture rather than the form that gives the temple its impact.

The friezes bring the building to life with the legends of the gods, Shiva the demon-killer, or scenes from the *Mahabharata*—including Prince Arjuna shooting a fish while looking at its reflection in an adjacent bowl of water. The bracket figures are masterpieces: a huntress, girls dancing or singing, and a woman about to spray her lover with rose-water. By the south doorway, on a vine chiselled beside the head of a girl dancing with a demon, you can find a lizard hunting a fly.

Hoysalesvara Temple in Halebid 16 km (10 miles) from Belur, dedicated to Shiva and his wife Parvati, is the biggest of the Hoysala temples. It suffered some destruction by the hands of Muslim iconoclasts, so it's worth visiting the **Archaeological Museum**, too, where some of the best of its statues are now kept. Look at the surprisingly fine carving of the bracket figures in the dancing hall, achieved by the craftsmen working with soft steatite soapstone which subsequently hardened to the texture of granite.

Sravanabelagola

Fifty km (30 miles) east of Hassan, the Vindhyagiri Hill rises 140 m (463 ft) above the plateau, with one of the most dramatic monuments in all India, the statue of **Gommatesvara**, on its top. To get to it, you must climb barefoot—the hill is holy ground—up 644 steps cut in the rock. Take it easy, and you'll find the trip well worthwhile.

Erected in A.D. 983, the statue crowns a sanctuary erected in the village of Sravanabelagola 1,400 years earlier by the Digambara sect of Jains, who regarded nakedness as part of the abnegation nec-

Gommatesvara was said to have stood in pratimayoga for a year: thus the creeping vine had time to wrap around his limbs.

essary to achieve true enlightenment (see page 22). It is believed that in the fourth century B.C. Chandragupta converted to Jainism at Sravanabelagola and fasted to death.

Coming upon the statue at the top of the hill, even though you may have already seen it from a distance, is still an awe-inspiring experience. This Jain saint looms 17½ m (57 ft) tall, carved from a granite monolith polished by centuries of libations with milk.

Gommatesvara, the son of the prophet Adinath, is entirely naked except for a single vine-creeper winding itself around his legs and arms. The creeper symbolizes the impassiveness he is said to have observed in this upright position of *pratimayoga*, which he adopted for one whole year in response to his brother's lust for worldly power. An anthill and serpents at his feet symbolize the mental agony that his smile shows he had conquered.

Duck herders guide their obedient flock down the wide, charming streets of Cochin.

Cochin

One of the most charming towns in India, where Christians, Jews, Muslims, and Hindus live in much greater harmony than they seem to manage elsewhere, Cochin makes a delightful gateway to the Malabar coast and the relaxed life of Kerala.

On a peninsula separated from the mainland by islands, the old part of the town is known as **Fort Cochin**, where Vasco da Gama set up Portugal's first Indian trading station. He was finally buried in the **Church of St. Francis**, the only Portuguese building still standing here. It has been subsequently converted by the Dutch to a Protestant church. The great navigator's remains were returned to Portugal in 1538 but his tombstone can still be seen on the south side of the church, set in the floor with a brass rail.

Keeping the Faith on the Malabar

The first Jews arrived here from Palestine on the Malabar coast, at nearby Cranganur, in the early centuries of the Christian era. Far from Roman persecutors, they traded peacefully with the Hindus or with Arab merchants from the Persian Gulf.

In time, their community was reinforced by new refugees from Babylon and Persia and then by others expelled from Spain and Portugal in 1492, spreading out along the coast. As luck would have it, however, the Portuguese settled there, too, bringing their Inquisition with them and upsetting the hitherto friendly Muslims. The Jews then promptly moved to Cochin, under the protection of the local Hindu raja. The Portuguese came down from Goa to smash the synagogue in 1662, but it was restored two years later. Today, with the last community fading away, there's no kosher butcher left in Cochin, but, as they say, what's wrong with vegetarian?

At the water's edge on the northern tip of the peninsula, you can see the fishermen's beautiful **Chinese dipping nets**, a system imported from the China seas: fishermen sling the nets over a pyramid of four poles which was then lowered into the water and hoisted out again by a system of rock weights and pulleys.

The **Jewish quarter**, referred to as "Jew Town," is in Mattancheri, south of the fort. In the narrow streets lined with merchants' and tailors' shops, the Star of David, *menorahs*, and Jewish names are actually more plentiful than Jewish people themselves. At Indian Independence there were a few thousand, but when the State of Israel was founded, a massive emigration left only dozens behind. The **Synagogue**, with its red tabernacle and Chinese tiling, was built in 1568. You can see the copper

Indian fishermen borrowed their system from the Chinese, hoisting tented nets in and out of the water with pulleys.

plates giving land rights to a Jewish community on the coast back in A.D. 379.

Take a **backwaters trip** through the lagoons and around the island villages. The local Government of India Tourist Information Office can help you rent a motorboat with a crew. You'll see fishermen working their dipping-nets or flinging hand-nets out with a whirling motion. On another island, women clean their shrimp at the water's edge; you can see the ecumenical peace of a church surrounded by palm trees, with a Hindu temple on one side and a mosque on the other.

On the way back, stop off at **Bolghatty Island** in the Cochin lagoon to take tea in the elegant Dutch governor's mansion, now a

hotel. Wildlife enthusiasts should visit the nature reserve at **Peri-yar**, a drive of 194 km (120 miles) from Cochin, where elephants, bison, and birds can be seen from the unique vantage point of an artificial lake. Look for the elephants with their trunks raised like snorkels. Take two or three days—anything less is likely to be a waste of time.

Kovalam

Trivandrum is a big town with an international airport—mostly for migrant workers going to and from the Gulf—15 km (9 miles) from the best **beaches** in India. Coconut palms, papaya, bananas, white

sand, and surf (beware of the strong currents) make Kovalam the ultimate in happy-go-lucky *dolce farniente*. It is not a temple, not a shrine or museum, and there's no palace in sight. Enjoy. For people visiting Kashmir who want to go on a trip down to the other end, India's southernmost point is **Cape Comorin** (two hours from Kovalam), where the Arabian Sea and Indian Ocean meet. There is nothing between you and Antarctica here. If your timing is right, you'll see the sea's bright colors when a full moon rises at the same time that the sun is setting.

In Cochin, disparate religions live together peacefully: here, the interior of a synagogue.

A trip by canoe through Cochin's lagoons is an excellent way to see its many island villages.

Madurai

The ancient capital of the Pandya kings and one of the world's oldest cities, Madurai is still an important repository of Tamil culture. Today it is a bustling university town, Tamil Nadu's second largest after Chennai.

The feverish religious activity around the 11 towering gopurams of the **Great Temple**, 17th-century in its present form, may give you a sense of the intensity of Hinduism. Its **Minakshi Devi Shrine** is dedicated to a pre-Hindu "fish-eyed goddess" taken into the pantheon with her husband, Shiva—his **Sundaresvara Shrine** is next door. The Madurai festivals in April and May celebrate their marriage as a grand reconciliation with the Indo-Aryan invaders.

Entering the temple, walk to the Minakshi shrine. Since the interior of the shrines is off-limits to non-Hindus, you can get a view of the entire temple and the golden roofs by climbing the slippery stairs to the top of the **south gopuram**. At ground level, you can see the arcaded **Golden Lotus Tank** and the temple's bathing-place. At the west end is a detailed model of the whole temple complex.

The **Kambattadi Mandapa**, the ambulatory to the Sundaresvara shrine, is the busiest place in the temple. Worshippers in procession prostrate themselves, bringing offerings of coconut and fruit, and toss tiny balls of butter onto blackened statues of Shiva. The **Hall of 1000 Pillars** (in fact only 997) is in the northeast corner, full of carved, bizarre lion-elephants, and the Pandava brothers, the heroes from the *Mahabharata* from whom the Madurai Pandyas claim descent.

Outside the eastern wall of the temple is the **Pudhu Mandapa**, the Hall of Audience of Tirumalai Nayak, who built the temple. It's now a bustling bazaar of tailors, metal-workers, and other artisans.

Stop off at **Tirumalai's Palace**, about a kilometer southeast of the Great Temple. An elegant relic of former splendor, the palace boasts cusped arches and massive pillars modeled on the style of the great Rajput palaces of Rajasthan, but also some unmistakably tubby Dravidian gods on a frieze running around the courtyard.

Trichy

The official, Indianized name of this town is Tiruchchirappalli, City of the Sacred Rock, but the place is still identified by its colonial name, Trichy, a short form of the equally European name Trichinopoly. Today it is a base for pilgrims visiting Tamil Nadu's great temple complexes, but every schoolchild, at least those from the old school, knew Trichy for the British defeats of the French here in the 1750s.

The famed **Rock Fort**, the main focus of these battles, looms over the city from atop the great solid granite hill that gave the town its name. From early days, the impregnable Rock served as a sanctuary, graced by temples and cave-shrines. Steep steps bring you up to the Hall of a Thousand Pillars, as well as the shrine of Shiva and the Temple of Ganesh, from which there is a fine view over the Cauvery river, the towers of Srirangam, and the plains beyond. On the way up, look for the seventh-century, stout-pillared Pallava cave-shrines.

The French have maintained their presence in Trichy, with the Jesuit College of St. Joseph and the adjoining red-and-buff Neo-Gothic church of Our Lady of Lourdes.

Srirangam

The numerous temple precincts of **Sri Ranganathaswami**, set on an island formed by two arms of the Cauvery river a few kilometers (3 miles) from Trichy, enclose a complete township of busy shops, booths, and dwellings. Beyond the town's outside wall are the temple's farmland and the coconut plantations—and a large, square, lotus-covered bathing tank.

The temple itself, dedicated to Vishnu and already a theological center by the 11th century, was founded a couple of thousand years ago—tradition takes it back to the Flood. Its present form comprises a total of seven concentric rectangular walled courts, culminating in an inner sanctum, and dates from the 15th and 16th centuries, after it had been liberated from Muslim invaders who had previously used it as a fortress. However, many of the sanctuaries are in fact much older than this.

Enter on the south side and proceed through an ornamented gopuram gate-tower characteristic of south Indian architecture. Next, pass under a series of soaring gopurams, where you can witness religion as a full-time daily occupation. The streets are crammed with vendors selling shrine offerings of sweets, curds, and coconut, as well as garlands and holy images. Elsewhere, men are cleaning the

Madurai's shrine to the fish-eyed goddess Minakshi is just one building in the temple-city at Srirangam.

stables for the temple elephants and the storehouses for the chariot-shrines that carry the deities through the streets during the festivals. Look out for the handsome pillared verandas of the dwellings.

Non-Hindus are allowed as far as the fourth courtyard. Here, on the south side, look for the shrine of **Venugopala Krishnan**, with its charmingly sculpted figures in the famous Hoysala style of the

temples at Belur and Halebid—notice the girl with the parakeet, which served in Indian literature as a bearer of messages between passionate lovers. Climb up to the terrace overlooking this shrine for an excellent **view** over the gopurams beyond the fourth court-yard to the golden vimana, the inner sanctum, and its arched roof with the god Vishnu portrayed on each side. Binoculars will be es-pecially useful here.

Most spectacular of all, though, set in the eastern courtyard of the fourth enclosure, is the **Sesharyar** worship hall with eight carved pillars of rearing horses bearing proud warriors. The energy of these minutely detailed sculptures from the 16th century, which honor the military prowess of the then-great Vijayanagar kingdom, is a zenith of south Indian art.

Thanjavur

Known to the British as Tanjore, this was the historic capital of the great Chola kingdom that spread Tamil culture to Burma, China, and Southeast Asia. Its artful sculpture and architecture can be seen to this day in the temples of Cambodia, Thailand, and Java.

Commercial enterprise, military power, and religious fervor went together. More than the divinity of Shiva, the 11th-century **Temple of Brihadisvara** boasts architecture celebrating the victory of the great Chola kingdom over the Pallavas of Kanchipuram and the Cheras of Kerala. The accent is on the grandiose: the temple's main vimana shrine consisting of a massive, 13-tiered pyramid some 66 m (222 ft) high.

Shiva's sacred bull, Nandi, is built on a similarly colossal scale, as is the phallic lingam, believed to be the biggest in India. Frescoes insist (in gory detail) that head-chopping was necessary to achieve victory. However, a much more graceful architectural touch can be

These men tap palm trees, drawing off the sap to be made into a potent fermented drink.

seen in the panels of Shiva demonstrating the 108 basic poses performed in the sacred dance, *bharatanatyam* (see page 206).

Chennai (Madras)

Chennai, known until 1996 as Madras, is easy-going, pleasant, and remarkably uncrowded. The beach here is an amazing 12 km (7 miles) long, but Chennai is also *the* place for banking and mailing packages, and for picking up letters from home at the *poste restante* counter of the General Post Office.

Chennai was set up in 1642 as the East India Company's first east coast trading station for shipping cotton and sugar. After the defeat of the French, it took a grateful back seat in Indian affairs, far away from the turmoils of northern India. These days, fiercely independent-minded Tamil politics make the place much more lively and alert at election time, but less heated than, say, the cities of Calcutta, Mumbai, or the Punjab.

Fort St. George is the home of Tamil Nadu's State government and the Indian Navy. There is a **Military Museum** and a British "relic" inside the Fort: **St. Mary's Church**, in the style of Wren. The most picturesque street in the old town, across the railway tracks north of the Fort (an area once known as "Black Town"), is **Armenian Street**. Still the center of a small Armenian community, there's a busy street market and, in a cool, tree-shaded garden, an open air colonnaded church.

The **State Museum** situated on Pantheon Road possesses excellent Buddhist bronzes and a detailed collection of Dravidian sculpture and architecture. From ninth-century Pallavas and Cholas to the rich style of the Vijayanagar kingdom (1336–1565), the exhibits make a fascinating demonstration in stone of the glory of south India.

The two main arteries of the city are the busy shopping center along Mount Road and Beach Avenue, where you'll find the University, Cricket Club, and **San Thomé Cathedral**. This simple, even

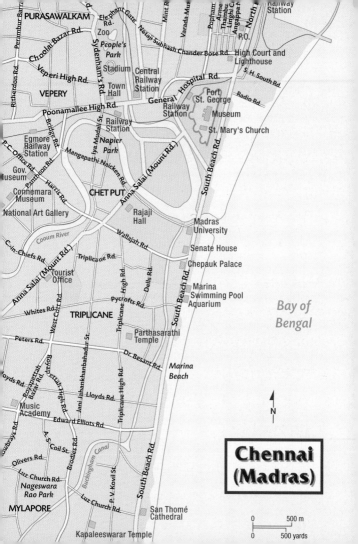

PURASAWALKAM

Elephant Gate Rd.
Zoo
People's
Park
Perambur Barracks Rd.
Choolai Bazar Rd.
Sydenham's Rd.
Veperi High Rd.
Mint St.
Netaji Subhash Chander Bose Rd.
Varada Mut.
Popham
Armeniam
Thambu...
Linghi C...
Angappa...
North...
Railway
Station
P.O.
High Court and
Lighthouse
S. H. South Rd.
Railway
Station

VEPERY

Ritherdon Rd.
Bridge Rd.
Town
Hall
Stadium
Central
Railway
Station
Poonamallee High Rd.
General Hospital Rd.
General
Railway
Station
Fort
St. George
Museum
Radio Rd.
St. Mary's Church

Egmore Rd.
Railway
Station
Napier
Park
Iya Mudali St.
Mangapathi Naicken St.
P-C Office Rd.
Gov.
Museum
Connemara
Museum
National Art Gallery
Pantheon Rd.
Harris Rd.
CHET PUT
Anna Salai (Mount Rd.)
South Beach Rd.
Cooum River
Rajaji
Hall
Wallajah Rd.
Madras
University
C-in-Chiefs Rd.
Anna Salai (Mount Rd.)
Triplicane Rd.
Tourist
Office
High Rd.
Dells Rd.
Senate House
Chepauk Palace
Marina
Swimming Pool
Aquarium
Whites Rd.
West Cott Rd.
Pycrofts Rd.
TRIPLICANE
Triplicane High Rd.
South Beach Rd.
Peters Rd.
Parthasarathi
Temple
Dr. Besant Rd.
Marina
Beach
Bay of
Bengal

Royal...
Royapettah
Bazar Rd.
Jani Jahankhanbahadur St.
Dereish High Rd.
Lloyds Rd.
Lloyds Rd.
Music
Academy
Edward Elliots Rd.
Triplicane High Rd.
N
A-S-Coil St.
Bombay...
Olivers Rd.
Bodlees Rd.
Buckingham Canal
Luz Church Rd.
Nageswara
Rao Park
MYLAPORE
P. V. Kovil St.
Luz Church Rd.
South Beach Rd.
San Thomé
Cathedral
Kapaleeswarar Temple

Chennai (Madras)

0   500 m
0   500 yards

austere Neo-Gothic Catholic church houses what is claimed to be the tomb of St. Thomas.

☞ Mahabalipuram

The ancient port of the Pallava kings, a high point in any tour of south Indian monuments, is only 60 km (36 miles) south of Chennai, but stay there overnight, rather than making a day-trip from Chennai, if possible. It has accommodations on the beach, enabling you to see the cliff-carvings, *ratha* shrines, and Shore Temple by the sea in the early morning and at night.

Originally the town was known as Mamallapuram, named after King Narasimha Mamalla (630–668), "the great wrestler," in whose reign its many extraordinary temples and shrines were begun. Like the cave-temples of Ellora (see page 118), most monuments are carved, rather than built, from solid rock, in this case the last cliffs and boulders of the vast granite plateau that ends at the Coromandel coast.

South of the village is a set of **rathas**, monolithic shrines hewn from one table of rock. Imitating elements of the region's wood-and-brick construction, some have the same arched and domed roofs as the

Ivy League Connection

Among the memorials to British heroes in St. Mary's, Americans may be pleased to see a plaque honoring the subsequent founder of one of its great universities, Elihu Yale, a former governor of the Fort. But Yalies have nothing to be proud of here. The merchant was fired in 1692 after five years as governor for amassing a large fortune under dubious circumstances while in the service of the East India Company. New England clergyman Cotton Mather, himself a Harvard man, got Yale to part with some of his ill-gotten gains to endow a new college that was to be named after him if he was the biggest donor. Yale sent a parcel of goods that sold for £562, and nobody did better.

Chennai's collective memory of its Victorian age is more serene than that of other big Indian towns.

inner vimana sanctuaries that you can see at Srirangam and at Thanjavur (see page 191). The largest shrine, the three-storied pyramidal **Dharmaraja**, at the southern end, has 50 figures, including gods, heroes, and, fascinatingly, modest subjects such as temple servants.

Of the rock-carvings north of the rathas, the most celebrated is **The Great Penance**. The narrative sculpture panels cover an entire cliff-face, in which a natural split in the rock has been assimilated as the Ganga river as it descends through the hair of Shiva.

The **Shore Temple**, which has withstood the wind and the waves for 12 centuries, is made up of two shrines. Shiva the Destroyer faces dangers at sea while Vishnu the Preserver watches over the town. The temple is clearly inspired by the styling of the monolithic Dharmaraja shrine, but it is more tapered because originally it had to double as a lighthouse, a bright beacon burning at its apex.

This exuberant bit of architectural detail proves that the British did not exert their influence over everything in Chennai.

Kanchipuram

Kanchi ("Golden City") has scores of temples—hundreds, if you include the shrines—dedicated to Vishnu and Shiva, and it is highly revered as one of the seven holy cities of ancient India. (The others are: Varanasi, Mathura, Hardwar, Dwarka, and Ayodhya.) It's an easy trip to make from Mahabalipuram and you can stop off to shop in Kanchipuram for silk.

Kailasanatha is one of the most important Shiva sanctuaries dating from the eighth century. The sandstone temple on a granite base houses some graceful sculptures of Shiva and Parvati as a celestial king and queen receiving homage from their subjects at their home on Mount Kailasa. **Vaikuntaperumal** is a Vishnu temple of the same period, famous for its elevated colonnade of lively sculpted reliefs showing the many exploits of the Pallava kings.

Pondicherry

The most visible Gallic touch in this bastion of the French colonial adventure in India is the scarlet *képi* worn by the white-uniformed traffic police waving you on as you drive into town. Many of the street names are still French—Rue Suffren, Rue Lauriston, Rue Dumas (Alexandre), and Rue Dupleix, today known as Rue Jawaharlal Nehru. However, only few people speak French here today. The French War Memorial on the coast road stands opposite a mon-

Doubting Thomas

When Jesus sent his disciples around the world to spread the Good Word, the disciple Thomas was told to go to India. "Whithersoever thou wilt, Lord, send me," said Thomas, as it is written in the Apocryphal Acts of the Apostles, "but to India, I will not go."

Then, Gondophernes, a Pallava king on the northwest frontier, sent for a master carpenter to help with the building of a new city. Thomas's professional pride overcame his hesitant evangelistic fervor and he realized it was an offer he couldn't refuse. He converted Gondophernes and proselytized throughout the south, covering the Coromandel coast, where he is said to have suffered martyrdom, and was speared to death while praying in a cave in the southwest corner of modern Chennai.

ument to Gandhi. After 250 years of French rule in Pondicherry, the Indians were fortunate to have the decolonizer Pierre Mendès-France to deal with when it was retrieved in 1954.

Apart from the pleasant white sandy **beach**, for nostalgics of the 1960s there's a pilgrimage to be made to the inspirational "Mecca," **Auroville**. This spiritual retreat, 10 km (6 miles) north

The people of Kanchipuram are equally proud of their stately temples and their superlative silk.

of Pondicherry, was started in 1968 by a French disciple of the teachings of the Indian sage, Sri Aurobindo. It lost some of its dynamism because of squabbles following the death of the founder, The Mother. But the "organic" forms of the buildings, with names like Hope, Fraternity, and Aspiration, still have an impact on the landscape. As Scandinavians and Bavarians cycle by, 1968 seems as remote as when the first cattle-herders came here from the other side of India some 3,500 years ago. The Dravidians were already here to meet them.

WHAT TO DO

SPORTS

One thing the Indians enjoyed about the British was their enthusiasm for sports—hockey and cricket in particular. In return, the British learned the delights of polo (imported with the Mughals from Persia and Afghanistan) and a kind of game-hunting that made grouse-shooting seem tame.

Today, with the exception of game-hunting, sporting life in India is still very active. Delhi in particular has very modern facilities, many built for the Asian Games in 1982. Just be careful to adapt your activities to the climate, and avoid going out in the midday sun.

Participant Sports

Swimming is a natural first choice. Many first-class hotels in leading cities have swimming pools, but there are a few precautions you should take when swimming elsewhere. For health reasons, it is best to avoid swimming in rivers, ponds, lakes, and reservoirs—your body is unlikely to be able to deal with some of the other things swimming around with you.

Beach swimming is best at the recognized resorts rather than at the major port cities. In Mumbai, both Juhu and Chowpatty beaches are, for instance, definitely a bad idea, and though the Marina beaches in Chennai are cleaner, there may be sharks. The best resort beaches are on the Malabar coast at Kovalam, Goa, and, smaller but charming, Cochin. Kovalam also has **surfing**, but be careful of strong currents. On the east coast, try Puri, south of Calcutta, or Pondicherry.

Sailing is possible at nearly all of the resorts. In Chennai, you can rent a catamaran and, if you're staying at the Taj in Mumbai, you should be able to obtain a guest membership at the nearby Yacht Club.

Fishing is very popular in India, and although it is almost entirely a freshwater proposition, you will find it very good. The indigenous mahseer, a distant relative of the carp, which can weigh as much as 20 kg (44 pounds), is considered by many sportsmen to be as good a sporting challenge as the salmon. You will find more information and fishing permits available at the Directory of Fisheries in the tourist office building in Srinagar. The tourist office in Delhi can provide information and permits for fishing in the Yamuna river and, similarly, the tourist office in Bangalore can be consulted if you wish to fish in the Cauvery river.

Hiking, or **trekking**, as it is most often called here, is a marvellous way of getting away from the often madding crowd in India, and you will find it is well organized in the old hill-stations.

A dip in a swimming pool such as this one will cool you down and satisfy any craving for a bit of glamour.

Travel agencies happily provide a range of camping and cooking equipment, as well as the guides, cooks, and porters you need, and a jeep for travelling to more remote and inaccessible areas. Try Simla, Darjeeling, Sikkim, and, much closer to Delhi, the Naini Tal region. The necessary arrangements for this can easily be seen to on the spot, but a more ambitious six- or seven-day trek needs some notice, so it would be best to book with your travel agent and settle the details before you leave home.

Golf and **tennis** fans will find these activities available in the major cities. Golfers should apply for a guest membership from the many clubs the Indians inherited from the British. Tennis lovers will find there are courts in the major hotels or in public parks.

Many of these hotels also have a health club with a **gym** or **yoga** class—the real thing.

Spectator Sports

The most beloved sport in India, by far, is **cricket**. There's something in the intricacy of its arcane rules and controlled passion that appeals to the Indian people. It's an astounding obsession—and all major cities have stadiums. The most fervent atmosphere of all is at the Calcutta Cricket

The beaches of Goa are renowned for their pleasant atmosphere and sparkling white sand.

Club, founded in 1792, five years after the Marylebone Cricket Club in London. The Brabourne Stadium in Mumbai is more relaxed. If you don't catch a major match, you may come across a competition in a Calcutta alley or a meadow in Kashmir.

Hockey is a British import, in which the Indians have surpassed their former masters. Today they often share the Olympic finals with their old arch-rivals, Pakistan.

Polo is a Rajasthani specialty, but tournaments are also held in Delhi and Mumbai in the winter months. This is a rich man's sport.

Horse-racing is popular, with races such as the Calcutta Derby, St. Leger, and the Oaks in Mumbai. The highest course in the

country is at Darjeeling. **Camel racing** is a big event at Jaisalmer in February and also in the autumn festival at Pushkar (see page 209).

ENTERTAINMENT

One of the many pleasant surprises in India is the way that its classical **music**—heard perhaps in snatches back in the West and often dismissed as something hopelessly beyond an ordinary Westerner's appreciation— grows on you when you hear it in the country of its creation.

A first encounter with Indian music is most likely to be in the pleasant surroundings of a restaurant in one of the major hotels (rather than in what might be the intimidating atmosphere of a large recital

These performers glide through the dramatic fire dance at Pushkar.

hall) where it may be performed as an accompaniment to an elegant dinner, with first-class musicians. The music consists of two basic elements: the *raga*, the melody of five or more notes, and the *tala*, the rhythm or tempo. Improvisation is of the essence. In a prelude or *alap*, which in full-length recitals can last half an hour, the lead musician seems to grope around until he reaches the main theme and its many variations take hold and patterns emerge from the apparent confusion. In its own way, it establishes a hold over you—soothing, lulling, and always fascinating—and before you know it, you're hooked.

Like the musicians themselves, give yourself up to the hypnotic effect of the notes, rhythms, and melodies, or even the silences. A fully realized performance could go on for two or three hours (shorter in restaurant recitals). It is perfectly normal at a concert for people to walk around, fidget, and talk at the beginning of the recital until the music asserts itself.

Apart from the music played in the big cities and the sophisticated music of the Brahmanic tradition, you can listen to the folk music of Rajasthan, rousing or plaintive, in the desert around Jaisalmer.

Song, using rhythm and melody in the same way as instrumental music, is religious and romantic in content. South Indian song is both joyful and sad. In the north, where song was subject to Arabian and Persian influences, it varies from *dhrupad*, meaning austere and

A circle of drummers and others play together at Trivandrum, in Kerala.

Weddings in India call for jubilant performance and celebration: here, wedding dancers congratulate the new couple.

without embellishment, to the more florid *khyal*, India's version of *bel canto*, or *thumri*, the style of light-hearted, tender love songs.

In addition to this dinner music, the major hotels organize full-scale recitals of music, song, and dance, and so if you do acquire a taste for it, look out for concerts in town—Delhi has recitals around Republic Day at the end of January.

Indian **dance** is marvelously expressive, with every gesture and movement signifying a vocabulary of emotions. Like the sculptures on the temples, the eloquence of dance is a means of transmitting the messages of the holy scriptures and adventures of the great Hindu epics to its listeners.

Classical sacred dance, *Bharatanatyam*, has a total of 108 different consecrated forms—you can see them performed by Shiva in the sculpted frieze of Thanjavur's Brihadisvara Temple (see page 191). Originally, these holy dances were performed by devadasis, the sacred dancing-girls, who were in fact the temple prostitutes—that is, until the Hindu reform movement during the 19th century made it acceptable for girls of respectable families to perform the dances, too.

In Kerala, try to see the lively *kathakali* dances, in which men play both male and female parts to enact both divine and heroic Indian legends in the most gorgeous costumes and elaborate make-up. Performances of musical works are regularly held in Cochin's neighboring town of Ernakulam. The more sophisticated dance found in eastern India is known as *Odissi*.

Sitar and Company

Indian music is played not by a full orchestra, but usually by two or three instrumentalists, all sitting crosslegged. One of the principal instruments, made famous in the West by Ravi Shankar, is the long six-stringed *sitar* with its bulbous sound-box. The robust *sarangi* is played with a bow, joined in the past couple of centuries by the Western violin, but played vertically, with its base held by the musician's bare right foot. The accompanist's four-stringed *tambura* provides the music's resonant ambience.

The ancient *vina*, a seven-stringed lute with a rounded body at the base and highly colored bowl at the top, was played by the goddess Sarasvati, muse of the arts, and just like the piano in the West, is played at home by respectable young ladies. The flute you'll see is essentially the same as the one used by the god Krishna.

There are two kinds of percussion: the small twin drums of the Indian *tabla* and the long bulging *mridangam* drum of south India, which is held horizontally, with the right hand providing a high-pitched tone for the melody and the left hand beating a deeper tone for the rhythm.

Festivals and Fairs

You could probably spend your whole time in India going to festivals. In a country with such a strong and varied religious tradition, and with people who are definitely inclined toward having a good time, there's always some reason for celebrating something. Here is a selection (the dates are loose because India follows a lunar calendar):

January: *Pongal,* in Trichy and Madurai; A three-day harvest festival during which cows and bullocks are fed with harvested rice. The atmosphere is generally jolly; the highlight is a variation on the bullfight in which young men try to pluck rupee notes from the horns of a very angry bull.

January 26: *Republic Day,* Delhi; Great march in which India shows off its cultural diversity and military might, the latter softened by a helicopter flying overhead disguised as a flying elephant with the pilot dropping rose petals on the crowd.

January/February: *Vasant Panchami,* throughout India but best seen in Calcutta; Honoring Sarasvati, goddess of scholars and artists. Everyone dresses up in bright yellow and flies kites. *Desert Festival,* Jaisalmer; A lively celebration of Rajasthani music and dance, plus camel races in the local stadium.

February/March: *Mardi Gras,* Goa; A hint of Portugal mixed with Indian. Costumes and dancing in the streets. *Shivratri,* Khajuraho and Varanasi; Solemn celebration of Shiva, with all-night music and prayers in the temples. *Holi,* northern India, best at Mathura The spring festival when lovers (and others) spray each other with colored powder and water.

March/April: *Gangaur,* Udaipur and Jaipur; Procession of girls balancing brilliantly polished brass pitchers on their heads with which they bathe Shiva's wife Parvati (Gauri). The garlanded deity is then accompanied by Shiva at the head of a parade of horses and elephants.

April/May: *Spring Festival,* Srinagar; Kashmiris bring out their samovars for a big tea party to celebrate the first pink-and-white almond blossoms, highlighted by mid-April festivities in the Mughal Gardens. *Baisakhi,* all over north India; The Hindus' solar New Year. The Sikhs celebrate the anniversary of Guru Gobind Singh's exhortation to form the khalsa ("army of the pure").

June/July: *Rath Yatra,* Puri; One of the greatest festivals of the year, when the three gigantic temple-chariots of Jaggannath, his brother Balabhadra, and sister Subhadra are drawn through the streets (see page 153).

July/August: *Amarnath Yatra,* Kashmir; During the full moon, thousands of pilgrims make their way from Pahalgam to the cave of Amarnath to Shiva's ice-stalagmite lingam.

September/October: *Dussehra,* Mysore, Delhi, and Calcutta; Ten days of pageant; elephant processions following behind the Maharaja of Mysore's throne. In north India, there is music, dance, and drama centering in Delhi on the legendary hero Rama (with fireworks blowing up his demon enemy Ravana), and in Calcutta on the goddess Durga.

October/November: *Pushkar Fair;* Camels, horses, and bullocks are brought to be sold at market. The camel races are spectacular; this is a fine place to buy Rajasthani craftwork. *Diwali,* all over India; The happiest of festivals honoring Lakshmi, goddess of prosperity (except in Bengal, where they honor their goddess Kali, immersing her in the Hooghly river).

November: *Sonepur Cattle Fair,* near Patna; On the banks of the Ganga, this month-long cattle and elephant market is one of the world's biggest, bringing all the usual colorful eccentrics into town.

December 25: *Christmas,* Mumbai and Goa; A more religious observance than in most Western countries.

Variable dates:
Muharram, Lucknow; Muslim mourning for Imam Hussein, grandson of Mohammed. Spectacular illuminated bamboo and paper replicas of the martyr's tomb are paraded through the town.
Id-ul-Fitr, Lucknow, Delhi, and Calcutta; Mosques are lit up as Muslims celebrate the end of the Ramadan fast.

Film in India, produced mainly in the cities of Chennai, Mumbai, Calcutta, and Bangalore, is a major industry. The large scale production of entertainment films is a phenomenon well worth seeing several times. You may well be more baffled by the appeal of the colorful musical comedies and violent shoot-em-ups than you would be in the West, but the emotion of the melodramas and romantic adventure stories of India's cultural and historic past have considerable curiosity value for a rainy afternoon. If you watch the action closely, you can learn a lot about Indian people by what makes them cheer, laugh, or weep. Calcutta seems to be the only other production center having any pretensions to artistic creativity at all, but ironically you're actually more likely to see the works of Satyajit Ray or Mrinal Sen shown in Europe or North America than in India itself.

SHOPPING

From the Greeks to the Turks and Mughals, from Marco Polo to Lord Mountbatten, all have been seduced by India's riches. It's still a great place to shop.

As in any ancient country, India's modernizing plunge into the 20th century has produced its fair share of trinkets and tinsel, but its traditional craftwork continues at the highest level: silks, carpets, jewelry, perfumes, brassware, and wood-carving are first class, and you will have the added bonus of dealing with the most charming bunch of merchants in the world.

At least half the pleasure is in the bargaining. If you don't want to be fleeced, don't plunge in blindly. Go first to the Government Cottage Industry Emporiums, which can be found in almost every major city. The selection here is not usually as wide as you'll find in the privately run shops and you can't haggle, but it'll give you an idea of the range of goods, the quality, and, above all, the correct price.

Then you're ready for the fray, either in the bustling great bazaars such as Delhi's Chandni Chowk or Mumbai's Bhuleshwar, or the more sedate ambience of grander shops and showrooms.

The one street market you shouldn't miss is Mumbai's Chor Bazaar, or Thieves' Market, which is an extravagant flea market where, among other things, you'll see Indian motorists buying back spare parts stolen from their cars the night before.

If, during your tours of the big cities, you come across products you like from places you will be visiting later, such as Rajasthan, Varanasi, or Kashmir, wait until you get there—the price and selection may be much better.

Haggling with dapper Gujaratis and the bright-eyed Kashmiris can attain the level of high art. Even if you don't land a bargain, there is real aesthetic pleasure in seeing, at the end of the verbal "combat,"

the disarray of silks thrown across a counter or a mound of carpets on the floor. The Kashmiris' wizardry is at its best on the floating market of their shikaras, but you can also meet Kashmiris down in the plains, to which, like many other wily birds, they migrate in the winter.

If there's no magic formula for the perfect bargain—each person will have his own psychological approach—you should avoid two extremes: Don't be too eager, and don't, on the other hand, assume everybody is out to cheat you. It spoils the sport.

Children get in on the cheerful act of decorating a puppet for the Diwali festival.

Carpets are one of the most attractive purchases you can make. Ever since the days when the Mughal emperor Jahangir took Persian craftsmen up to Kashmir with him during his long summer holidays, the handwoven silk-and-woolen carpets of Srinagar have been among the best in the world. The silk gives the carpets their unique sheen. The prices will vary according to the proportions of silk and wool used and the density of the weave itself; naturally, none of these pieces are cheap.

Look out for traditional Persian and original Kashmiri motifs such as peacocks and fruit trees, tiger hunts, and Mughal lovers. Indeed many of the carpets seem just too lovely to walk on, but they make superb wall hangings, and even if you can't remortgage your house to buy a big one, even a modest bedside rug can do wonders to warm and brighten a room.

This Bangalore produce market is overflowing with a bounty of fresh fruit and vegetables.

Cashmere is the one thing the Kashmiris are touchy about. That "100% cashmere" label you show them on your best sweater could provoke a loud snort of "Scotland!" or even "Australia!" But then, like an endearment to a beloved one, they will murmur "*pashmina*" and spread before you a shawl of soft, warm wool shorn, they tell you, from the underbelly of the wild Himalayan goats. Then, just when you think you've never touched anything finer, they turn around and whisper "*shahtoosh,*" laying out the finest Kashmir wool of all, taken from the throat of the ibex and woven so finely that one can pass a shawl right through a wedding ring. These, too, are expensive, but you can get shawls of good quality wool with distinctive embroidery at more reasonable prices.

Silks have long been basic to a fine Indian lady's wardrobe and also make magnificent tunics, blouses, stoles, or long, trailing scarves for a Western outfit. The costume more easily adapted to Western tastes than the sari, perhaps because it involves trousers, is a long tunic worn over baggy pantaloons with a soft stole around the shoulders; known as *salwar kameez,* it is most popular in the northwest, and very elegant.

Three towns are famous for their silk: Bangalore, for its classic printed silk; Varanasi, for its gold and silver brocades; and Kanchipuram, for its heavy, brilliantly colored silk, favored for formal saris. Not forgetting the men, the city of Kanchipuram also produces superb silk ties.

Cottons, either hand-printed or embroidered, are probably the best bargain of all Indian textiles, made into tablecloths, napkins, bed linens, spreads, pillowcases, and airy, light scarves that make life much more comfortable in the Indian heat. Indian tailors are cheap, good, and fast, so you might consider having lightweight shirts and baggy pants made up for you during your stay.

Three cotton prints to look out for, particularly in Rajasthan, are: *bagru,* consisting of geometric or fish, almond, and vine patterns in blue, brown, and maroon; *sanganeri,* block printed floral and paisley patterns; and *bandhani,* tie-dye, which results in decorative color. The bright motifs with mirror-work stitched into them, much favored by Rajasthani ladies of the desert for their long flowing skirts, are known as *cutchhi* or *saurashtra.* The dashing, rather coarse cotton Punjabi *phulkari* shawls are made from fabric with patterns in orange, pink, green, red, and yellow.

Jewelry is important here, whether made with precious or semi-precious stones. The jewelry of Rajasthan is much sought after. Indian diamond mines produced some of the world's greatest gems, including the Kohi-nur (Mountain of Light), now in the British crown jewels, having originally been set in the Peacock Throne. Although the mines are superseded by those in South America and South Africa, the art of cutting and polishing is still extant in Gujarat. Mumbai is a center for importing rough-cuts and selling the finished product. Don't buy any unless you are an expert or have one

with you. Diamonds are graded from D to X, with only D, E, and F considered good, D being colorless or "river white," J "slightly tinted," Q "light yellow," and S to X "yellow."

The essential piece of jewelry in India, however, is the bangle. Whole stalls are devoted to them, made from silver and gold, metal, wood, glass, plastic, and—best bargain of all—colorful varnished papier mâché from Kashmir.

Gold, silver, copper, and brass—each has its own bazaar in the big neighborhood markets of Delhi, Mumbai, and

There are many different types of lovely Indian textiles to consider for your purchase.

Calcutta. Of these, the most well known is Jains' Zaveri Bazaar in Mumbai, where antique gold is sold.

Wood carvings vary from rosewood elephants or sandalwood camels to the Kashmiris' finely fretted walnut, created in the style of the screens on the Srinagar houseboats.

For modern painting, try the art galleries around Connaught Place in New Delhi and Mumbai's Pundole and Chemould Galleries, not to forget the Academy of Fine Arts in Calcutta.

Cooks should be on the lookout for spices—chili, turmeric, cardamom, ginger, nutmeg, and cumin—which we advise you not to buy until your last day. The best places to buy Indian spices are the

Indian pottery, though sometimes overlooked for the more well-known crafts, often makes an excellent souvenir.

Khadi Bhandars, because they are government supervised, thus offering a product of assured quality.

Tea gourmets will make a beeline for Darjeeling, to buy directly from the plantations or at the town bazaar. When you buy a couple of kilos, they'll ship it for you in air-tight packages.

EATING OUT

India's fine cuisine is as rich and diverse as its civilization—and home-cooking is best. Big hotels and first-class restaurants will, however, allow you the opportunity to taste various regional dishes.

The dishes are highly seasoned, but the spices are subtle; it will take some time for you to get used to the flavors, even if you're familiar with Indian cuisine back home. Although hotels are at pains not to overdo the hotter spices, it's still likely to be much sharper than you will be used to. So, take it easy—a little at a time. You should not expect each day to be a major culinary adventure. Even if your tastes are very simple, you may be quickly bored by the food in the more modest establishments and smaller towns.

On the other hand, it would be silly to steer away completely from local food. It's unlikely that you came to India to eat the same food that you're used to back home. In any case, Indians are much

*Your dining experience in India can be as luxurious—
or as simple—as you like.*

better at cooking Indian food than they are at preparing what the menu calls "Continental" (i.e., bland all-purpose Western meals). Few hotels break the beef taboo to serve steaks or hamburgers, though you may find some made from buffalo meat.

Breakfast

All the trimmings of British and American breakfasts are usually available: porridge (oatmeal), cereals, eggs, and bacon, with tropical, fresh seasonal fruits such as mango, papaya, and pineapple, and their juices.

One Lump or Two?

The tea planters in Darjeeling are snobs with something to be snobbish about. Their aromatic tea is India's best; in its purest form it is horrendously expensive, but understandably so, when they get an average of 400 kg (550 pounds) per hectare, compared with some 1,340 kg (3000 pounds) down in the plains, although this may improve with new methods of scientific "cloning."

Darjeeling's dainty "China" tea—as opposed to Assam's coarse, broad-leafed variety—is taken from the top of the bush, just two leaves and a bud, and taken away to the factory, where it is then withered and rolled, fermented, dried, and graded. Here, planters never use the "curl, tear, and crush" method (CTC for short)—in fact, veteran Darjeeling planters prefer not to even speak of CTC—which is what the tea planters do down in the plains.

The quality of Darjeeling's tea grades is reflected in the poetry of their names: Golden Flowery Orange Pekoe, Golden Broken Orange Pekoe, Orange Fannings, and Dust, which is used for tea bags.

By the way—unlike the British practice, which is regarded as barbarian, the local connoisseurs who do add milk do so after, not before, pouring the tea.

Coffee in north India is usually instant, but do ask for the excellent Madras brew wherever it's available. Tea is rarely Darjeeling, but you'll find the Assam type is as good as any in British hotels. For safety's sake the milk is boiled, then re-cooled for the cereals.

Indian-style breakfasts may be rice and curried vegetables with a drink of *lassi*, cold liquid yogurt, either sweet or seasoned with salt or cumin. In the south, you'll find *idli*, *dosa*, and *hoppers*—different forms of rice- and lentil-flour pancakes—which may be folded around mixed, mildly spicy vegetables like a crêpe and served with fruit *chatnis*.

The cuisine of India is based on several mixtures of savory and delicate spices.

Lunch and Dinner

If you have plenty of things to do in the afternoon, keep lunch light and plan your gastronomic adventure for around 8pm to give yourself plenty of time to digest. Hotels will often provide large buffets, giving you a chance to try several dishes, which people tend to pile up on one plate around a large mound of rice. But traditional Indian meals are served on a *thali*, a large metal platter, with each dish in a separate little bowl, *katori*, so that you can savor the different tastes separately.

Places that have assimilated the British custom will serve a soup like mulligatawny—which is a spicy chicken, mutton, or vegetable broth created for colonial officials. Otherwise, with the exception of the food served at great banquets, meals are not divided into courses; everything will usually arrive on your thali at the same time.

You'll find it good to follow the Indian custom of drinking something either before or after, but not during, a meal. Drinking does not in the end alleviate a peppery flavor because it will leave your taste-buds completely defenseless against the next hot mouthful. Therefore, it's better to eat some plain rice or one of the soft Indian breads, fruit, or, best of all, yogurt.

Indians eat with their fingers, rotating the finger tips around the plate to form the food into a ball with rice or bread. Cutlery may be provided, but a fork is not necessarily any more hygienic than fingers.

"Curry"

Properly speaking, there's no such thing as a curry. It's a British term invented to refer indiscriminately to India's spicy preparations of fish, meat, and vegetables. It has been traced to the Tamil word *kari*, meaning quite simply "sauce." In India there is not one "curry powder" or "curry sauce," because each dish has its own combination of spices.

The Spice of Life

You may be pleased to know that, according to the ancient canons of Indian medicine, the myriad spices in your meal are all working to improve your health. While the combination stimulates the appetite and helps your digestion in this very special climate, some of the individual spices have surprising properties.

Turmeric is very good for skin ailments, ginger for your liver and rheumatism. Cloves can help the kidneys, relieve fever, and also stimulate the heart. Coriander fights constipation and insomnia, but one of the most versatile is cardamom, battling bad breath, headaches, throaty coughs, and hemorrhoids.

The utensils and the stove here are modern, but the chapati recipe is as old as India itself.

The combination of spices commonly used in a basic mixture of sautéed onions and garlic is called *garam masala*, a powdered blend of coriander, cumin, ginger, black pepper, cinnamon, pimento, cardamom, bay leaves, cloves, and nutmeg. Saffron adds its own unique color and fragrance, both to rice and to meat. In fine establishments, saffron is even used to perfume the room before the meal begins.

Non-Vegetarian

The classical cuisine of the north, *mughlai*, comes from the Mughals. With beef taboo for Hindus and pork for Muslims, the meat is lamb or mutton, its classic "curry" being *rogan josh*. Cubes of meat are prepared in a yogurt sauce made with chili, ginger, coriander, and garam masala. This dish originated in Kashmir, where they eat lamb in dozens of different ways (if you attend a *wazwan* banquet, there may be as many as 16, 36, or even 52 dishes.).

If you're a home-chef, drop in on one of India's bazaars for some spices and other souvenirs.

Other dishes are the *kebab*, balls of lamb minced with almonds and spices; *tabakmas*, mutton ribs with a crispy skin; and *goshtaba*, the most tender lamb from the breast, with every last sinew beaten out of it before it is minced into a fragrant dumpling stewed in yogurt. In Kashmir this is the climactic dish of a wedding banquet —after eating the liver, the kidneys, the shoulder, the leg, and various minced kebabs.

Biryani is a Mughlai specialty, originally exclusively a lamb dish, though chicken, fish, and vegetables are now cooked in the same way. This dish is more elaborate than *pulao*, which is a simple mixture of rice and lightly flavored meat or vegetables. Biryani is chicken or lamb cooked in a sauce of ginger, cardamom, cinnamon, and cloves, before steaming it with saffron rice and *ghee* (clarified butter). It may be served decorated with almonds and mint—and with a thin film of edible but tasteless silver, which adds luxury to the dish.

Chickens tend to be scrawny, but they are tasty in a *makhni* butter sauce, as *murg ilaychi*, marinated in yogurt with cardamom, ginger, peppers, and saffron, or *murg do pyaza*, with shallots and onions. *Tandoori* chicken is a popular barbecue in the northwest style, baked in a *tandoor* clay oven. Typically, the chicken is salted and doused in lime juice, tenderized with papaya, then marinated in yogurt with a flavoring of ginger, garlic, chili, and saffron, before being plunged on a spit into the charcoal-heated oven. Fish and giant prawns, marinated in different sauces, also make very good tandoori dishes.

Rice and Chapatis

The best rice is the aromatic long-grained basmati, the common or garden variety known as *patna*. Apart from biriani and pulao, north Indian

---

Goa For Gourmets

This old Portuguese colony, with a large Christian community, holds a unique position on the country's gastronomic map. Happy to use pork and beef in its very spicy "curries" and pungent sausages, it also makes splendid use of the abundant seafood available off its Malabar coast.

Tisryo is a delicate dish of tiny stewed clams, spiced with ginger and sprinkled with coconut. But Goa's most celebrated dish, the "Goanese curry," is a thick sauce of tamarind, coconut, onions, and tomatoes, served over a variety of local seafood such as clams, shrimp, crab, and anything else the fishermen have caught that day, all of it spiced to the gills. It's the Sunday lunch, but there's usually enough for a whole week. You probably won't have room for an *alebele*, a sweet and spicy crêpe stuffed with coconut. Save that one for Monday, and eat it with with the potent *feni*, a fermented cashew drink.

---

cuisine does not feature large quantities of rice as does south Indian cuisine. The Indians in the north prefer to eat their food with a variety of breads, including a floppy, thin *roti* or *chapati*; a slightly thicker *paratha*, sometimes stuffed with vegetables or minced meat; small deep-fried *puri*; or giant puffed-up *nan*, baked in a tandoor. Here's a tip: before you tackle the rice dishes of the south, try eating with your fingers in the north by folding a piece of roti around each morsel.

Vegetarian

Favorite vegetable dishes, or *sabzi*, are *aloo gobi* (cauliflower and potato), *bhaingan bharta* (roasted eggplant), *sag panir* (mustard leaves with Indian cottage cheese), *bhindi* (okra), *channa* (chickpeas), and *dal* (lentil soup).

In addition to the fresh seafood cooked and eaten, particularly in the kitchens of Goa, the cuisine of southern India is more vegetarian than that of the north. This is because the region was not subject to the Mughal influence. Whereas the north cooks with the products of its cattle, such as ghee for frying, yogurt for sauces, and milk for desserts, the basis of southern cooking is the coconut—its oil is used for frying, and the milk and flesh for sauces. This gives the food a sweeter taste than in other regions. Sauces, in which water, vinegar, or coconut milk is added to the spices, are gradually absorbed by the rice as the meal progresses.

Side-dishes and Snacks

Salads don't exist in the Western sense, but *cachumbar* is a refreshing side dish of tomato and onion seasoned with fresh lemon juice or vinegar. The great palate-cooler, eaten both in the north and south, is *raita*, a mixture of cold seasoned yogurt and either cucumbers, potatoes, tomatoes, or pineapples.

As a sweet condiment, Indians serve not only mango, but mint and coconut, fresh ginger, tomato, dates, or even tamarind in a spicy *chatni*. You'll find that some of the flavors in these dishes pack an astonishing double punch of sweet and sharp.

There are some wonderfully tangy Indian snacks. Mumbai's best is the *bhelpuri* sold on Chowpatty Beach (see page 126), a spicy snack made from fried chickpeas and noodles. *Samosas* are stuffed with meat or vegetables and *pakora* is a vegetable fritter. *Pani puri* is a small pastry stuffed with spiced tamarind water, so you should put the whole thing in your mouth at once.

Desserts

Ras malai are patties made from cottage cheese and nuts, sweetened with aromatic syrup, and perfumed with rose water and cardamom.

Khir, rice pudding, invented in India with condensed milk and broken rice, mixed with cardamom and nuts, is much superior than its British counterpart. *Gajar halwa*, a dessert of grated carrots stewed in milk and syrup, is best hot, with raisins and nuts. *Kulfi* is ice cream made with cardamom and pistachio. *Barfi* and *halwa* are sweets made with flour or milk and flavored with nuts and fresh cardamom.

Drinks

The most cooling drinks are *nimbu pani* (water with fresh lime) and fruit juices, especially from the fragrant Kashmiri apple. Indian beers are acceptable, white wines drinkable, and whisky tolerable.

European wines are exorbitant and, frankly, not good to drink with curry anyway. Among traditional Indian alcoholic drinks are palm toddy in Kerala; *asha*, a rice beer from the Himalayan foothills; and a meat-based liqueur made in Rajasthan. In Goa people drink *feni*, a cashew-based liqueur.

> ## Very Fishy
>
> The strictest vegetarians exclude fish, meat, poultry, and eggs, and even blood-colored vegetables such as beet or tomato, quoting the ancient Sanskrit verse: "In the next world animals will eat those who eat them in this world." Some Brahmins of Bengal do eat fish, calling them "fruit of the sea."

INDEX

HANDY TRAVEL TIPS

An A–Z Summary of Practical Information

A

ACCOMMODATION

Indian tourist accommodation caters to all tastes. There are luxury hotels in big cities as well as in all major centers of tourist interest (such as Agra and Jaipur). In former princely states, ancient maharajas' palaces have been converted into hotels, those in Rajasthan being very successful. Some have been taken over by large commercial groups; others are run by members of princely families. In most cases, however, their popularity has caused a rise in prices. In old "British India," at cheaper rates, you can find the hotels of yore. There are numerous smaller but comfortable establishments at much lower rates throughout the country.

If you are not travelling in an organized group or have no reservation, you should head straight for the local tourist office and consult the list of "government-approved" hotels, which guarantees minimum standards in terms of facilities and also of general hygiene.

If you land when tourist offices are closed, you will find that in almost every town, government-run **tourist bungalows**, **hotels**, or **lodges** provide satisfactory accommodation, where the rates vary according to the comfort sought, such as whether the rooms have air-conditioning and hot water.

Every locality also has a **rest-house** or **dak-bungalow**, which often constitute the best value for money in India, but you may need to bring your own bedding. Book these in advance from the administration's local head office (either the public works department or the local authorities), or you can simply turn up on the doorstep and be given a room. It is best not to chance your luck in tourist centers like Agra or Jaipur.

Most railway stations have **rest rooms** where you can stay for a night or a few hours. They are clean and cheap; you must hold a valid railway ticket to qualify for one. Most establishments will ask you whether you want "AC" rooms (air-conditioned) or "non-AC." From May to September it is wise to spend a few rupees more to enjoy a cool retreat.

Be wary of the water in the plastic flask near your bed. Water shortages and power cuts, frequent in summer, do not allow automatic discounts. In the cheaper hotels, check your bed-linen and do not hesitate to have it changed if necessary.

India

Officially, all foreigners are expected to pay their hotel bills in foreign exchange. This, however, is only really applicable to luxury establishments, since few others have access to the day's rate of exchange.

YMCA and YWCA hostels (couples, married or not, are accepted) are in every large town and provide adequate, often excellent, accommodation.

AIRPORTS

The international airports in Delhi and Mumbai welcome the bulk of tourists and visitors to India. Airports at Calcutta and Chennai are also equipped to receive international flights.

Indira Gandhi International Airport, New Delhi, is located 20 km (12 miles) southwest of the city. The terminal facilities include a buffet and a number of currency-exchange counters, as well as a luggage deposit facility, hotel reservation, car rental, and pre-paid taxi counters, and a duty-free shop.

Sahar International Airport is situated 29 km (18 miles) north of the city center. This is by far India's busiest airport, both for international and domestic services. Its international terminal (Sahar), which is based over 5 km (3 miles) away from the domestic terminal (Santacruz), but linked to it by a regular shuttle-bus service, has all the facilities of a modern airport. At peak hours, the journey from the center to the airport can take three hours, so allow for transfer time.

Arrival (see also CUSTOMS, ENTRY, AND EXIT REGULATIONS). On arrival you will be required to fill in a Disembarkation Card. These are generally distributed to passengers on board the plane. Visitors who do not have any dutiable goods, high-value articles, foreign exchange in excess of US$1,000, or unaccompanied baggage, all of which have to be declared, can simply walk through the Green Channel. Others however, will have go to the Red Channel for the appropriate clearance.

Ground transport. Airport terminals are organized to provide you with a cheap bus ride into town at regular intervals, and throughout the night if the airport is a busy one. Airport bus services can be found in smaller places. You are also assured of finding taxis and motor-rickshaws. Taxi-runs from the airport are based on set fares which will naturally vary from airport to airport. Convenient pre-paid taxi services operate in all the major cities. Elsewhere, a policeman at the gate will ask for your name and destination (he isn't prying, he's simply curbing taxi-driver greed). You will also be given a complaint card with a telephone number you might want to keep handy. Taxi fares to destinations in town are generally posted on signs near the airport taxi stand.

Departure. On leaving India, you will be required to pay an airport tax in rupees. Security checks at airports are particularly intensive.

ALCOHOL

Only one state in India, Mahatma Gandhi's home state of Gujarat, remains completely "dry." Alcohol is generally available elsewhere, except in very remote areas and in religious centers. The once compulsory All India Tourist Permit is no longer necessary. Some hotels will ask you to drink either in your room or in the hotel's licensed bar — but it's up to you to shake off the guilt complex. Other than luxury hotels, few restaurants are authorized to serve beer or other alcoholic drinks. The first and seventh of each month are dry days (no alcohol will be available anywhere) in Delhi, and the first and tenth in Mumbai. The days vary from state to state.

B

BUDGETING for YOUR TRIP

The following are some prices in Indian rupees and US dollars. However, they must be regarded as approximate, due to inflation.

Airport departure tax. Rs500 (Rs150 to neighboring countries).

Car rental. Charged per km from Rs3 to Rs6 for a non-air-conditioned car; from Rs7 upwards for an air-conditioned (AC) Indian car; more will be charged for a luxury imported vehicle; Rs30 to Rs40 per hour waiting charges. Overnight charges for the driver start from Rs100 per night. Remember that all rented cars are chauffeur-driven. In the cities a car may be rented on a flat rate basis (e.g., 4 hours or 40 km Rs200 non-AC; Rs300 AC).

Cigarettes. Rs35–50 for a packet of 20.

India

Discover India Pass. 21 days US$440.

Hairdresser. From Rs70 for a man's haircut in a luxury hotel; from Rs175 for a woman's shampoo and cut.

Hotels. Double room in a luxury establishment Rs2,000 to Rs6,000 per night. Middle of the range hotels from Rs1,000 to Rs1,700 per night for a double, depending on whether it is air-conditioned or not. Local and luxury taxes are extra, approximately 5–20%, although this can depend on the state in which you are travelling.

Indian Airline Discount fares. The Discover India Pass is valid for 21 days and costs US$440.

India Wonder Fare. 7 days US$200 (see page 253). Youth fares have a 25% discount for anyone under 30.

Indrail Pass. US$150 for 7 days first class, US$530 for 90 days first class.

Meals. A snack: Rs40 upwards in a middle-range restaurant; from Rs100 in a luxury hotel. Full meal (Indian style): from Rs150.

Taxis. Fares to and from airports are supposed to operate at a fixed rate. Motor-rickshaws start from Rs per km; the fare is double or triple for taxis.

Trains. Delhi to Mumbai (approximately 1,400 km/1000 miles) AC first class Rs2577, non-AC first class Rs943, AC second class Rs1470, non-AC second class Rs262, AC chair car Rs750.

C

CIGARETTES, CIGARS, and TOBACCO

Tobacco products with Indian brand names are on sale everywhere. Some international companies manufacture their brands in India. Most people find Indian cigarettes acceptable. Indigenous pipe tobacco and cigars are not always easily available. If you are a compulsive smoker, try the bidi, a single leaf of tobacco rolled and filled with shredded tobacco.

The Sikh religion places a ban on smoking, so you'll be asked to hand in all your tobacco at the entrance when visiting a *gurdwara* (Sikh temple).

CITY TRANSPORT

Taxis exist in all large cities. **Tourist cars** (chauffeur-driven) can be rented out in centers of tourist interest through the local tourist office. Other than airport-to-hotel journeys, which operate on a fixed fare, all drivers must use their meters. Meters, however, are generally out of date, and the driver will show a conversion chart for the fare.

Motor-rickshaws, also known as scooter-rickshaws (three-wheel mini-taxis) operate in a similar way. Again, fare rates vary from town to town; in general, a scooter-rickshaw fare is about half a normal taxi fare. Scooter-rickshaws are banned in Mumbai's congested inner city zone, so you must use a taxi, bus, or suburban train.

In all big cities, there is an efficient **bus** service which, when you know how to use the route guide available from all bookstalls, is convenient. The only problem is that buses in India carry large crowds.

There are also **cycle-rickshaws** and *tongas* (horse-drawn carts), for which you agree on the price before starting off. Calcutta and a few other places still have old-style **rickshaws** pulled by men. Calcutta also has India's first **metro** (either subway or underground) line (clean, cool, and the pride of Calcutta) and India's last operating **tram** service (less crowded, slow and cheap).

CLIMATE (see also pages 60–62)

India can be conveniently divided into three zones — the north, the south, and the hill regions — and into three distinctive seasons: the winter, the summer, and monsoon. The best time to plan your trip to India is from mid-September to early April, except for the hill-stations, which are good at any time in the summer except during the monsoon.

The monthly average maximum and minimum daytime temperatures* in degrees Fahrenheit are:

		J	F	M	A	M	J	J	A	S	O	N	D
Mumbai	max.	83	83	86	89	91	89	85	85	85	89	89	87
	min.	67	67	72	76	80	79	77	76	76	76	73	69
Calcutta	max.	80	84	93	97	96	92	89	89	90	89	84	79
	min.	55	59	69	75	77	79	79	78	78	74	64	55

India

Delhi	max.	70	75	87	97	105	102	96	93	93	93	84	73
	min.	44	49	58	68	79	83	81	79	75	65	52	46
Chennai	max.	85	88	91	95	101	100	96	95	94	90	85	84
	min.	67	68	72	78	82	81	79	78	77	75	72	69

And in degrees Celsius:

Mumbai	max.	28	28	30	32	33	32	29	29	29	32	32	31
	min.	19	19	22	24	27	26	25	24	24	24	23	21
Calcutta	max.	27	29	34	36	36	33	32	32	32	32	29	26
	min.	13	15	21	24	25	26	26	26	26	24	18	13
Delhi	max.	21	24	31	36	41	39	36	34	34	34	29	23
	min.	7	9	14	20	26	28	27	26	24	18	11	8
Chennai	max.	29	31	33	35	38	38	36	35	34	32	29	29
	min.	19	20	22	26	28	27	26	26	25	24	22	21

* Minimum temperatures are measured just before sunrise, maximum temperatures in the afternoon.

COMMUNICATIONS (see also HOURS)

Telephone and **telegrams.** India is in the process of modernizing its telephone system, raising great hopes for the future. In the meantime, however, many city numbers, particularly in Delhi, Mumbai, and Chennai, are being altered to suit new telephone exchanges. Before calling, check whether the exchange code, the first few digits in the number, are still correct.

Direct dialing is possible between major cities. Where you make a call through the operator, you'll have to book a few hours in advance.

The inter-city telegram service is frequently disrupted by line failure. Public telex is often the best way of reaching another part of the country.

For international calls, extensive satellite links can connect you with almost anywhere in the world with a service up to international standards.

You can book both domestic and international telephone calls through the hotel switchboard or at the nearest PTO (Post and Telegraph Office), or use the direct dialing booths. There are also privately operated International Subscriber Dialing/Subscriber Trunk Dialing (ISD/STD) facilities, where a meter will record the duration of your call; you pay the proprietor the required amount when you have finished. Big cities have a 24-hour telephone and telex service at the central PTO. India also has reverse-charge (collect-call) agreements with most countries.

Postal service. The postal service within India and abroad is generally very reliable. An airmail letter usually takes up to seven days to Europe or the US. Stamps are sold at post offices and in some large hotel receptions. It is best to watch your letters being franked rather than using public letter boxes. Lower denomination stamps and envelopes tend not to stick very well, hence the pot of glue on all counters. You can send bulkier souvenirs home by surface mail, but you must first have the package cleared by customs. The Speed Post service for internal mail is quick (most letters are delivered within 24 hours), cheaper than a courier, and very reliable. This service is also available for sending letters and parcels to a few foreign countries (destinations vary from one post-office to another). International courier services are available in larger towns and cities.

CRIME and THEFT

One wouldn't expect to recover a camera left on a park bench anywhere in the world, and India is no exception. However, your valuables are probably less at risk in India than in many parts of the West. Common sense precautions go a long way: don't leave valuables lying around, and avoid being obvious — a few hundred dollars are a year's earnings to many people.

Violence against foreigners is virtually unknown in India, and it is probably safer to walk through Delhi late at night than many places back home.

CUSTOMS, ENTRY and EXIT REGULATIONS

Visas. All travellers, including Americans and citizens from Commonwealth countries, need visas. There are three kinds of visa: *entry*, *tourist*, and *transit*.

Entry visas apply to those frequently travelling to India on business assignments; they can be extended.

Transit visas, with a maximum duration of 15 days, are only needed if you are just making a stop-over and want to leave the airport. They are granted to passengers who have tickets for onward destinations. Two-way transit visas can also be obtained.

Tourist visas are normally valid for three months and can only be extended at the Government's of India's discretion. You must arrive in India within six months of the visa date of issue, or it will automatically become void. For a tourist visa, you will need four passport-size photos. Unless you

India

hold a passport from a fee-exempt country, you will be expected to pay for your tourist visa. Tour organizers can arrange for group visas.

Arrival (see also AIRPORTS). Tourists are allowed to bring in all the usual paraphernalia they normally carry. Certain high-value items, however, will be entered in your passport by the customs officials, but if you are thinking of returning to India on the same passport, insist that the customs officers cancel these entries. Any items which have been written into passport cannot be sold and must be shown on departure. In case of loss or theft, you will need a police document which proves that you have reported the incident.

Firearms and habit-forming drugs are banned and so is the import of gold bullion and electronic items for commercial purposes.

Departure. When leaving India, you are allowed to take all kinds of souvenirs, provided they are not recognized antiques (this is defined as any items which are over 99 years old) — it is always best to keep your sales receipt with you to appease any over-zealous customs officers. Please note that you may not export any kind of animal skin other than a small amount of cow leather and a few peacock feathers. You should steer clear of tiger-skin rugs and snake skins.

The following chart shows the allowances made for certain duty-free items that you may take into India and, when returning, into your own country. Check them out before you leave, rather than running into any major problems at than airport.

	Cigarettes		Cigars		Tobacco	Liquor		Wine
India	200	or	50	or	250g	1l		1l
Australia	250	or	250g	or	250g	1l	or	1l
Canada	200	and	50	and	900g	1l	or	1l
Ireland	200	or	50	or	250g	1l	and	2l
N. Zealand	200	or	50	or	250g	1.1l	and	4.5l
S. Africa	400	and	50	and	250g	1l	and	2l
UK	200	or	50	or	250g	1l	and	2l
US	200	and	100	and	*	1l	and	1l

*A reasonable quantity

Currency restrictions. It is forbidden to take Indian rupees into or out of the country. There is, however, no limit set on the total amount of foreign currencies you can bring into India, providing you declare amounts in excess of US$2,500 on arrival. Foreign currencies that total the amount imported and declared may be exported.

E

ELECTRIC CURRENT

Electricity supply in all tourist areas and big cities is a standard 220 AC, 50 cycles. Only a few remote parts of northern India are still using DC. The voltage can fluctuate wildly, especially during the summer months, so avoid plugging in delicate systems directly without the use of a voltage stabilizer. Power failures can also occur, so consider taking some spare batteries with you just in case.

EMBASSIES, HIGH COMMISSIONS, and CONSULATES

Most countries have diplomatic ties with India, with an embassy or high commission in New Delhi and a consulate in Mumbai, Calcutta, or Chennai.

Australia	*High Commission*: 1/50 Shanti Path, Chanakyapuri, New Delhi 110021; Tel. 6888223
	Consulate: Maker Towers, "E" Block, 16th Floor, Cuffe Parade, Colaba, Mumbai 400005; Tel. 2181071/72
Canada	*High Commission*: 7/8 Shanti Path, Chanakyapuri, New Delhi 110021; Tel. 6876500
	Consulate: 41-45 Maker Chambers, VI, Fourth Floor, 6 Jamna Lal Bajaj Marg, Nariman Point, Mumbai 400021; Tel. 2876028/29
New Zealand	50-N Nyaya Marg, Chanakyapuri, New Delhi 110021; Tel. 6883170
UK	*High Commission*: Shanti Path, Chanakyapuri, New Delhi 110021; Tel. 6872161

India

| | *Consulates*: Maker Chambers, IV, First Floor, 222 Jamnalal Bajaj Marg, Nariman Point, Mumbai 400021; Tel. 2830517. |

Consulates: Maker Chambers, IV, First Floor, 222 Jamnalal Bajaj Marg, Nariman Point, Mumbai 400021; Tel. 2830517.

1 Ho Chi Minh Sarani, Calcutta 700071; Tel. 2425171.

24 Anderson Road, Chennai 600006; Tel. 8273136/37

US   *Embassy*: Shanti Path, Chanakyapuri, New Delhi 110021; Tel. 6889033

Consulates: Lincoln House, 78 Bhulabhai Desai Road, Mumbai 400026; Tel. 3633611 and 3633681.

5/1 Ho Chi Minh Sarani, Calcutta 700071; Tel. 2421218 and 2423611.

220 Annar Salai, Chennai 600006; Tel. 8273040

G

GETTING TO INDIA

Due to the complexity and variability of the many fares, you should ask the advice of an informed travel agent well before your departure.

Scheduled Flights

All major international airlines land at Delhi and Mumbai (see under Airports); some also fly to Calcutta and Chennai. Approximate flying times: London–Delhi 11½ hours; New York–Delhi 19 hours.

Charter Flights and Package Tours

From North America: India is featured on a number of tours from the United States, many of them combined with another country such as Nepal, China, or Japan. There are a number of package tours from Canada.

From the United Kingdom: A wide variety of tours is offered, with air/hotel packages to Mumbai, Calcutta, Delhi, Goa, Jaipur, Kovalam, Chennai, and Udaipur. There are also tours available that take in two or more Indian cities and that combine India with another country such as Nepal or Sri Lanka.

From Australia and New Zealand: India is sometimes featured on Asian tours, but these are not frequent.

Overland

It is possible to cross into India by land from both Nepal and Bangladesh, but the journey can be somewhat strenuous — by bus from Kathmandu to Dehli, or by bus from Dhaka to the Bangladesh border, then by train to Calcutta. Both routes take a minimum of two or three days. After recent turmoil in the western state of Punjab, foreigners were prohibited from traveling by land from Pakistan, but the restriction has since been lifted.

H

HEALTH and MEDICAL CARE

Before travelling to India, you are advised to take out a personal health insurance policy to cover possible mishaps. Most insurance companies provide this service.

Likewise, consult your family doctor for a routine check-up and ask him to prescribe medication for potential stomach upsets. Anti-malaria tablets must be taken at least two weeks before departure and for six weeks upon returning home. Remember also to pack a small bottle of light wound disinfectant.

Most people during the course of their stay in India will contract some form of stomach trouble. In most cases, it is nothing to worry about, being more irritating than anything else. The remedy is simple: avoid rich, spicy food for a while, double-check drinking water (be sure to avoid tap water), peel all the fruit you eat, and take medication if required. Bottled mineral water is widely available in the cities, but may be difficult to obtain in the smaller towns. Stock up whenever possible.

Due to the dramatic weather changes between seasons, people can catch heavy colds at any time to the year. Carrying tablets that combat flu symptoms will help. Dust may cause conjunctivitis, so soothing eye drops will come in handy. Sensitive skin also needs to be protected against the sun. Bring insect repellent and an anti-irritant for insect bites. High levels of heat can cause outbursts of prickly heat (use talcum powder) and migraines. Take plenty of liquids and mineral salts to combat dehydration.

India

Although not mandatory, vaccinations against tuberculosis, hepatitis, and tetanus may be worth it. A valid yellow fever certificate is mandatory for those from South America, Africa, and other areas where yellow fever exists.

While in India, steer completely clear of stray mammals — particularly dogs — because there is a risk of rabies.

Cities like Delhi and Mumbai have Western-style clinics; your embassy in New Delhi can recommend one. Government hospitals are cheap, but if you are going to have injections done here, insist that the doctor either uses a disposable needle or that the sterilization process is done in front of you; this is for your own peace of mind.

HOURS

All central government offices, except post offices, railways, etc., follow a five-day week, closing on Saturdays and Sundays.

Most **markets** close one day a week; the day varies from place to place. **Shops** generally open at 10am and close by 8pm; some are shut for lunch.

Administrative **offices** (other than central railway and airline offices) only start becoming active by about 11am; they will be devoid of life by 5:30pm. The official lunch break is from 1:30 to 2pm. Station booking-counters open with the first trains.

Banks dealing with foreign currency open from 10:30am to 2:30pm on weekdays, and from 10:30am to 12:30pm on Saturdays. However, on Saturdays it may be difficult to change your travelers' checks outside the main cities.

Post offices open at 9:30am, closing at 5:30pm in larger places and 3:30pm elsewhere. Getting there early to avoid the crowds isn't always the best idea — you might have to wait some time for the staff to arrive. In major cities, the main telephone and telex office generally provides round-the-clock service.

Museums and **parks** are open until 5 or 5:30pm, but you should check which day they stay closed.

Hairdressers in large hotels will take clients in the early evening.

L

LANGUAGE (see also USEFUL EXPRESSIONS)

Hindi, based on Sanskrit and akin to many European languages, is the official national language of India, but each state also has its own regional language — one of the 15 listed in the Constitution. English is still used alongside Hindi for official purposes.

People in north India generally speak Hindi, while in the south, where the regional languages are Dravidian, you'll find more English spoken.

M

MAPS

Good road maps of the Indian subcontinent are published in Europe, and the US Indian tourist offices hand out useful maps and brochures.

Street maps are not always available, but your best bet will be the local tourist office or your hotel reception desk. Street maps of big cities like Delhi and Mumbai can be purchased from newspaper stands, but they are a little misleading sometimes.

MEETING PEOPLE

All transactions and most social encounters in India begin with the well established ritual of exchanging visiting cards. Like everywhere else, politeness in India is considered to be a virtue. You'll quickly find that most Indians will go out of their way to be friendly and helpful to you. A traveller will frequently be asked about his nationality, name, marital status, and children, though the limited spread of English tends to restrict the scope of most conversations to simple things. It can be a bit tedious to go around like a walking curriculum vitae, but just keep smiling. This quaint curiosity is built on the best of friendly intentions, and it is part of India's charm.

No topics of conversation are taboo, providing you don't take up an intransigent or arrogant stand. On the contrary, Indians are extremely eager to explain their country and their beliefs to foreigners, which could make for interesting conversation.

India

Indians seldom shake hands when greeting people, other than during the course of official business; instead, you'll soon learn to *namasté* with both hands brought together at face level.

Many Indians do not drink and/or are vegetarian, so if you are inviting someone out for a meal, it would be a good idea to inquire beforehand about tastes and preferences.

MONEY MATTERS (see also Hours)

Currency. The Indian unit of currency is the *rupee* (abbreviated *Re*), which is divided into 100 *paise*. There are coins of 5, 10, 20, 25, and 50 paise, and of 1, 2, and 5 rupees (*Rs*). Banknotes exist in denominations of 1, 2, 5, 10, 20, 50, 100, and 500 rupees.

Indians are rather fussy about the condition of their paper notes. A shopkeeper often turns down a note because it is very slightly torn at the edge while accepting another one with a great big hole in the middle! There is a very much mistaken belief that the Reserve Bank of India has ruled that notes which are torn at the edge are worthless. In fact, the Reserve Bank has a special counter for accepting or exchanging torn or soiled notes, and most other banks will do the same. However, they may refuse to do so if you don't bank with them. So check your change carefully every time you pay for something, and refuse any frayed and dirty notes. Don't try to mend notes with transparent sticky tape — they become unacceptable this way.

There is a chronic shortage of small cash and many shopkeepers give out sweets or stamps by way of change. Taxi and motor-rickshaw drivers are also notoriously without adequate change; you might often find yourself having to pay a little more just to break up a roadside deadlock. When cashing in your foreign exchange in a large bank, it would therefore be a good idea to ask to have part of your Indian money given to you in small notes. Some banks give extremely valuable wads of a hundred notes of Rs1 or 2. Hang on to the bank receipts, since these will allow you to cash in your excess rupees on departure. Note that it is a criminal offense to change money on the black market.

Travelers' checks can be cashed in at most banks and in many hotels, though in the latter case it may be at a slightly inferior rate. Some shops are also authorized to deal in foreign exchange.

Credit cards and personal checks. Use and acceptability of credit cards is becoming increasingly widespread in India now. All big hotels and government emporiums recognize them, and so do many shops and restaurants. Personal checks, however, will find few takers, although some foreign banks will help you out, providing you can produce a foreign resident in India who will stand as surety.

N

NEWSPAPERS and MAGAZINES

English-language newspapers, both national and regional, are widespread throughout the country. There is a large number of English-language news magazines, some of which are absolute musts for those interested in the intricacies of Indian political and social life. Most of the major cities now have a weekly *What's On* type of magazine (available from bookstalls), which gives the opening and closing times for museums and information on current cultural events.

P

PACKING

While most things are easily available in large Indian towns, there are still certain items you'll be relieved to have with you.

Other than essential medicines (see HEALTH AND MEDICAL CARE), think of packing in your luggage the following items: a drinking-water bottle; a pocket torch (flashlight); a padlock if you are thinking of staying in a few cheaper hotels (digital padlocks spare the worry of losing the key) or if you are going to travel a lot on Indian railways; a penknife (but don't board planes with it in your cabin luggage); water-purifying tablets; a money-belt; and half a dozen passport size photos of yourself — which come in useful if you are applying for permits to Darjeeling or Sikkim or for a rail pass. A universal plug for wash basins will come in handy more often than you might imagine.

Aspirin and mosquito repellent are readily available, but you might like to have your own favorite brands handy. Also, don't forget to pack some sterile cotton wool and adhesive bandages, and last but not least, toilet paper or paper tissues (found only in large Indian towns).

Sewing kits can be useful, but in every hotel there will be somebody to do the job for you; if not, on every sidewalk there is at least one tailor or one cobbler capable of performing instant miracles for a few rupees.

Pack a cloth hat to protect against the sun, as well as sensible light cotton clothes to wear during the hot and monsoon seasons, a swimsuit, and a pullover for cold spells during the winter months or trips to the hills (see also CLIMATE).

When travelling long distances by rail, a bedsheet can make a lot of difference to your comfort, and so will a plastic or aluminum mug, which will allow you to drink tea you bought on the platform when the train moves off. Ear plugs can sometimes be a life-saving device, particularly at night in crowded compartments, or in a bus with non-stop Indian film music (often distorted) blaring out of the public address system. A short-wave transistor radio will enable you to keep in touch with world affairs.

Finally, you might also like to bring with you a few small gifts for people who have been particularly helpful and shown you hospitality. Any small item with a foreign trademark on it will be happily accepted; this could be disposable gas lighters, ball point and colored felt-tip pens, stamps from your own country, cigarettes, picture postcards, perfume samples, etc. In many places you might find yourself surrounded by swarms of children clamoring for "school pens, stamps, and coins."

PHOTOGRAPHY

Color and black-and-white film is readily available in the main cities, but film for slides is not easy to find in India. Some shops in big cities do stock E6 preparations (Agfachrome, Fujichrome, etc.) but retail prices are about three times what they are in Europe.

Delhi, Mumbai, and other larger towns have plenty of photo studios that can process black-and-white or color film. Generally the quality is good, but prints are usually postcard size only. It is perhaps best to take the film back home with you to have it processed there.

Customs impose a limit of five rolls of film per person. Although all metal detector machines are said to be film-safe, you might feel happier, when passing airport security checks, to carry your film in a clear plastic bag, handing it over to the security staff for inspection.

India is a colorful country, and your finger will be itching on the shutter trigger of your camera from the moment you arrive. There are, however, certain things which can't be photographed: military installations, bridges of all sorts, airports and railway stations, power stations and refineries, dams, and telephone exchanges. Likewise, it is always best to get permission to photograph any person.

PLANNING YOUR TRIP

Most of India is open to foreign travel, with the exception of the territories of Assam, Arunachal Pradesh, Nagaland, Manipur, Mizoram, Tripura, and Meghalaya. Some of these areas are open to organized tours, but not to individual tourists. Information on restrictions may be obtained from Tourist Information offices. There is also an "inner-line" exclusion zone running along the frontier between India and China. People wishing to trek in Ladakh, as well as parts of Darjeeling and Sikkim, should inquire at the local tourist office before setting off: some hill areas may be completely open, others may need special access permits (see page 162), and others still will be entirely out of bounds.

Though the government of India places no restrictions on travel in Kashmir, most foreign consulates warn against travel in this region, due to incidents of extreme violence against foreign travellers in recent years. Those considering Kashmir as a destination should check with their country's consulate in Delhi before proceeding.

The FRROs (Foreigners Regional Registration Offices), which can be found in Delhi, Mumbai, Calcutta, Chennai, and other state capitals, come under the umbrella responsibility of the Under Secretary, Home Affairs Ministry, Foreigners Division, Lok Nayak Bhavan, Khan Market, New Delhi 110003. They will be in charge of all visa and permit problems.

POLICE

Traffic police do not carry guns. However, uniforms (on the colorful side) generally vary from state to state. Police forces responsible for law and order are armed, the officers with revolvers and the rest with Enfield rifles. Banks are guarded by armed, retired servicemen. Each locality has one or more police stations or police booths where foreigners can register any complaints they may have.

PUBLIC HOLIDAYS

Due to the many religions in India, public holidays are plentiful and confusing. Fixed national holidays are set on the following dates: 26 January, Republic Day; 15 August, Independence Day; and 2 October, Mahatma Gandhi's Birthday. Banks are closed on 30 September and 31 March. Other holidays vary according to region. A list of official holidays can be obtained from tourist offices.

R

RADIO and TV

All India Radio (AIR) broadcasts on medium wave, with news either in English, Hindi, or a regional language.

Indian television provides news in Hindi and English, as well as an array of indigenous films, song and dance programs, farming and science reports, and sport. Imported films, documentaries, serials, and sports programs are also broadcast. Luxury hotels generally provide a TV set in each room.

RELIGIOUS SERVICES

No other country in the world has such a wealth of faiths as India, reflected in the beautiful architecture of its churches, mosques, and shrines.

Access to places of worship is generally open, except for some Hindu temples and all Parsi fire-temples. Mosques are closed to non-Muslims at certain times of day. In most places of worship you'll be asked to take off your shoes and/or cover your head, so it might be a good idea to take along some form of head-covering. You'll find Sikh *gurdwaras* ban the entry of tobacco, while Jain temples forbid anyone entering the premises to bring in any form of leather (including wallets). Therefore, if you wish to take advantage of all the opportunities for sightseeing, you should consider packing a hip bag or money belt made from canvas or another fabric that would be acceptable.

Synagogues can be found in big cities such as Mumbai and Delhi; Christian churches of all kinds exist in practically every town.

RESTAURANTS

First-class hotels naturally offer sophisticated surroundings and a touch of luxury for the traveller. There is no fool-proof way of sorting out the better restaurants before actually sampling the food. Trial is still the best method for judging standards.

Many of the small roadside establishments, not exactly enticing by some Western standards of conviviality, sometimes serve excellent fare for next to nothing, but these are not recommended for the short-stay traveller.

On the Menu

aloo	potato
barfi	sugar and milk sweets
biryani	north Indian rice and meat dish
chai	tea
chapati	unleavened bread cooked on an open pan or griddle
chawal	rice
dal	lentils or kidney beans
faluda	sweet noodles with milk and ice cream
gosht	meat, generally mutton
halwa	carrot- or semolina-based dessert
idli	little dumpling of steamed rice flour, eaten at breakfast with chutney and curry
kebab	barbecued meat
keema	minced meat, generally mutton
kirra	cucumber
kofta	spicy minced-meat balls
korma	a curd-based curry sauce
kulfi	Indian ice cream
lassi	curd-based milkshake, sweet or salty
masala	mixed spices
masala dosa	pancake of rice flour and ground lentils with spicy potato filling
mutter	peas

India

nan	leavened bread
nimbu pani or nimbu soda	fresh lime with water or preferably soda
pakora	deep-fried savory fritter with onion or potato
paneer	Indian cottage cheese
papad/papadum	crispy spicy wafers
paratha	flaky chapati, generally fried in butter and often stuffed
pomfret	type of very fleshy fish
pulao	north Indian rice and meat dish
puri	deep-fried "bubble" chapati
raita	curd (*dahi*) mixed with either tomatoes, green peppers, cucumbers, potatoes, or pineapple
roomali roti	paper-thin chapati ("roomal" means handkerchief)
roti	generic name for oven- or pan-cooked bread
sabzi	vegetables
sag	mustard leaves
samosa	deep-fried, stuffed pasties
seer	type of very fleshy fish
tandoori meat	(generally chicken) marinated in spice and curd, cooked in a traditional oven
tikka	pieces of diced meat/fish, marinated and grilled on an open fire

T

TIME DIFFERENCES

Indian Standard Time (IST) is GMT plus 5½ hours, winter and summer alike. The most bizarre time difference in the world exists between India and Nepal: 10 minutes!

	New York	London	**Delhi**	Sydney
January	1:30am	6:30am	**noon**	5:30pm
July	2:30am	7:30am	**noon**	4:30pm

TIPPING

It is customary to leave a tip of about 10% of the total bill in restaurants. Elsewhere, however, tipping is entirely discouraged by the Government of India. Do not try to tip government employees, although museum guides will invariably give hints at the end of a conducted tour, so it will be up to you to decide whether his stories and information are worthy of a tip. In temples, however, it's a different story: the baksheesh is more or less mandatory. You should also give a rupee to the person who looked after your shoes while you were visiting.

TOILETS/RESTROOMS

The toilets in India are generally very, very basic, but all the same, don't shun the "eastern" (seatless) version, because they are often much more hygienic than the European style. The water tap (faucet) nearby is to wash afterwards. Tourists will often bless their stock of paper tissues.

TOURIST INFORMATION OFFICES

Indian Tourist Offices at these addresses will help prepare your trip:

Australia: Level One, 17 Castlereagh Street, Sydney, NSW 2000; Tel. (02) 232-1600 and (02) 232-1796

Canada: 60 Bloor Street West, Suite No 1003, Toronto, Ontario M4W 3B8; Tel. (416) 962 3787/88

Japan: Pearl Building, No. 9-18 Ginza, 7 Chome, Chuo Ku, Tokyo 104; Tel. (03) 571-5062/63

UK: 7 Cork Street, London, W1X 2AB; Tel. 0171-437 3677/78

US: 1270 Avenue of the Americas, Suite 1808, New York NY 10020; Tel. (212) 586-4901 or 1-800-953-9399; fax (212) 582-3274.

3550 Wilshire Boulevard, Suite 204, Los Angeles, CA 90010; Tel. (213) 380-8855

In India the major tourist offices are:

Mumbai: 123 Maharishi Karve Road, opposite Church Gate; Tel. 2033144/45.

Santacruz Airport; Tel. 6149200. Sahar International Airport; Tel. 8325331

India

Calcutta:	4 Shakespeare Sarani; Tel. 2421402 and 2425813. Dum Dum Airport; Tel. 5118299
Chennai:	154 Anna Salai; Tel. 8522139. Meenambakam Domestic Airport; Tel. 2340386. Meenambakam International Airport; Tel. 2345801
New Delhi:	88 Janpath, New Delhi 110001; Tel. 3320005, 3320008, and 3320109. Indira Gandhi International Airport; Tel. 3291171. Domestic Airport; Tel. 2295296

Generally, airport tourist offices are open 24 hours; others 9am to 6pm.

TRAVELLING AROUND INDIA (see also page 63)

Air (see also AIRPORTS). India has an extensive airline network, although flights can sometimes be unreliable. The main problem is booking; many of the more popular routes are full months in advance. Don't waste time on arrival: as soon as you know where you are going and how you want to get there, book. There are two types of ticket: *confirmed*, which are (mostly) trouble-free, and *requested*, which frequently offer only a slim chance of travel.

Indian Airlines (IA), the state-owned domestic carrier, offers tourists two discount schemes: a 7-day *India Wonder Fare* (one region only) or a 21-day *Discover India* fare, with unlimited travel but only one stop in each town. The *Discover India* tickets must be purchased abroad either at Air India offices or at an agreed travel agent. The *India Wonder Fare* can be obtained in India, but must be paid for in foreign currency. Tourists are expected to pay for their tickets in foreign exchange.

In Delhi, the IA office is at Safdarjung Airport; Tel. 4620566 and 4631337. In Mumbai: Air India Building, Nariman Point, Mumbai 400 021; Tel. 2896161.

There are a number of private airlines operating throughout India, offering a good standard of service, which are well worth considering. There are also various companies in operation which run air taxis linking up smaller towns, particularly useful if you are thinking of going to some of the more remote hill-stations.

Rail. Indian Railways (administratively divided into Northern, Western, Eastern, Central, and Southern railways) have five basic classes of travel: First Class Air Conditioned (AC), Second Class AC, AC Chair, First Class non-AC, and Second Class non-AC. During the summer months an AC compartment is best, especially if travelling through the Indian plains.

Other than a few super-deluxe fast trains, there are three types of train: *Express*, *Mail*, and *Passenger*. You should certainly avoid *Passenger* trains, which stop at every station no matter how long the journey.

Tourists will find the *Indrail Pass* the best buy if they intend to use the train a lot. These are valid for unlimited travel for 7–90 days. Pass holders have a priority booking allowance at most stations. *Indrail Passes* can be purchased abroad through approved travel agents. You can buy them in India from approved travel agents and at special railway-station booking counters for tourists in Delhi, Mumbai, Calcutta, Chennai, Goa, Bangalore, Varanasi, Agra, Ahmadabad, Aurangabed, Chandigar, Gorakhpur, Hyderbad, Jaipur, Trivandram, Amritsar, Rameswaran, and Vadodara.

All long-distance trains have sleepers. Second Class non-AC berths are wooden planks; First Class and AC berths are cushioned. Second Class berths, whether AC or not, give straight onto the main corridor, but First Class berths are separate compartments with slide-doors and catch-locks. In First Class and AC, you can rent sheets and blankets (nights can be chilly in AC, even in the summer).

Bring plenty of books, fruit, and drinking water. You will marvel at the ability of Indian travelers to emerge from a 48-hour journey as fresh as when they started, while you will be in dire need of soap and water.

Food is served on Indian trains. Apart from one or two luxury trains, there won't be much of a choice (generally it will simply be a question of vegetarian or non-vegetarian). Meals will generally consist of a thali or a cardboard box filled with plastic bags of curry and rice.

Foreigners need their passports for booking tickets.

Road. Where there's no railway (e.g. parts of Rajasthan), there will be a road and dozens of inter-city buses. The fares are low, and so is the comfort. Buses on routes like Agra and Srinagar are plush and classy. Discovering India by car is best, and cars are rented chauffeur-driven.

U

USEFUL EXPRESSIONS

Hindi is spoken mainly in the north of the country. Here are some useful words and expressions to listen out for and use. Verbs ending with a "-yé" sound are polite imperatives, but those ending with a "-o" are familiar forms of address. The "-ji" suffix is a polite honorific. A wavy line over a vowel indicates a nasal sound.

Yes	ji hã
No	nah
Please	meher bāni
Thank you	dhanyavād (sometimes "shukriyā" in northern India)
My name is….	Mera nam…hai.
What is your name?	Apka nam kya hai?
Beg your pardon/sorry	māf (or shama) kijiyé
Hello/welcome/goodbye	namasté
How are you?	kyā hāl hai/āp kaisé hai
I'm fine.	thik haĩ
I don't understand.	samjhā nahĩ
Tomorrow/yesterday	kal (confusion is possible)
Today	āj
Tonight	āj rāt ko
This morning	āj subhā
This evening	āj shām ko
Good	achchā
Excellent/well done	shābāsh
Fast/early	jaldi
Slow/late	dhiré
Money	pāisā
How much is it?	kyā dām hai
It is very expensive.	yé bahut mahinga hai
Are you free? (taxi, rickshaw)	kyā āp khāli hai
How far is it?	kitni dūr hai

Where is it?	kahã hai
On your right	dãy
On your left	bãy
Straight ahead	sidha
Please stop here.	yahã rokiyé
Please go faster.	jaldi chaliyé
Please go slowly.	dhiré chaliyé
Please go away.	jãiyé
Go away!	jão
Let's go!	chalo (polite form chaliyé)
Please bring	lãiyé
Please give	dijiyé
I'm not feeling well.	mai kuchch bimãr hũ
I need a doctor.	mujko doctor chaiyé
This is not good.	yé achchã nahihai
It is very good.	bahut achchã hai
It is very hot.	bahut garam hai
It is very cold.	bahut thandã hai
It is very beautiful.	yé bahut sunder hai
Please give me some water.	mujko pani dijiyé
This is not clean.	yé saf nahi haĩ

The following two are fairly important since they are not only typically Indian but also occur frequently in the press, and on official documents, etc.

100,000	lakh (written: 1,00,000)
10,000,000	crore (1,00,00,000)

NUMBERS

1	ek	10	dass
2	do	11	gyarah
3	tin	12	barah
4	char	20	bis
5	panch	30	tis
6	chhé	40	chalis
7	sat	50	pachãs
8	ath	60	sãth
9	nau	70	sattar

| 80 | assi | 100 | sau |
| 90 | nabbé | 1000 | hazar |

W

WEIGHTS AND MEASURES

India uses the metric system everywhere.

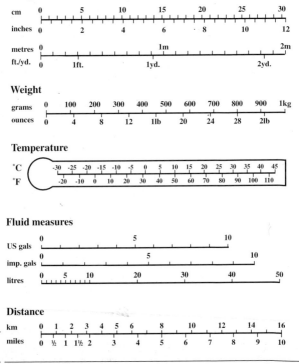

Length

cm 0 — 5 — 10 — 15 — 20 — 25 — 30

inches 0 — 2 — 4 — 6 — 8 — 10 — 12

metres 0 — 1m — 2m

ft./yd. 0 — 1ft. — 1yd. — 2yd.

Weight

grams 0 — 100 — 200 — 300 — 400 — 500 — 600 — 700 — 800 — 900 — 1kg

ounces 0 — 4 — 8 — 12 — 1lb — 20 — 24 — 28 — 2lb

Temperature

°C -30 -25 -20 -15 -10 -5 0 5 10 15 20 25 30 35 40 45

°F -20 -10 0 10 20 30 40 50 60 70 80 90 100 110

Fluid measures

US gals 0 — 5 — 10

imp. gals 0 — 5 — 10

litres 0 — 5 — 10 — 20 — 30 — 40 — 50

Distance

km 0 1 2 3 4 5 6 8 10 12 14 16

miles 0 ½ 1 1½ 2 3 4 5 6 7 8 9 10